THE ART OF ANCIENT MEXICO

THE ART OF
ANCIENT MEXICO

109 PHOTOGRAPHS BY
IRMGARD GROTH-KIMBALL

TEXT AND NOTES BY
FRANZ FEUCHTWANGER

THAMES AND HUDSON – LONDON · NEW YORK

THE ART OF ANCIENT MEXICO

HERNÁN CORTÉS' expedition of conquest, an undertaking of world-wide significance, was aimed with astonishing accuracy at the heart of the native civilizations of Central America. The manœuvres of his fleet prior to the landing at Vera Cruz, upon which he set his seal by scuttling the ships, show how systematically the white conqueror and inheritor of the Aztec realm reconnoitred the foreign coasts before deciding to stake everything upon a single throw: his rapid march to the Valley of Mexico and against Tenochtitlán, the present-day Mexico city. The enterprise proved as successful as it had been daring. Within two years the Aztec capital was firmly in Spanish hands. This meant that by 1521 Cortés controlled a territory stretching from the Pánuco river in the north to the border of what is now Guatemala; at the same time certain neighbouring provinces which were not under Aztec rule, namely the so-called Kingdom of Michoacán in the north-west and the areas to the south inhabited by the Maya and Quiché peoples, fell easy prey. Twenty years later the conquerors held this large territory under their sway, whereby they suppressed the natural customs of the indigenous population and made them subject to a Catholic-ridden Spain which was already moving toward a mercantile system based on colonial exploitation.

At no other point on the new continent would it have been possible for these entirely alien worlds to have encountered one another with such dramatic and far-reaching results. True, Cortés and his men still believed themselves to be on the trail of a fabulous India and did not appear to be surprised to find, in this unknown land, admittedly alien yet basically familiar conditions: a political structure, a network of cities, market centres, trade routes and a people subject to a rigorous social code and adept in many crafts; in short, an empire which could be taken over. How differently they would have fared had they set foot upon the mainland north of the twenty-second parallel or on the Caribbean coast deep in the south, beyond what had since ancient times been the zone of highly developed civilizations, and where at the beginning of the sixteenth century the Aztecs were the decisive power! These unique civilizations had invariably been built up and succeeded one another in this same area—a comparatively narrow strip of land which joins the two American continents.

It is still a matter for speculation as to when the first inhabitants of America, who according to current opinion reached North America from Asia via the Bering Strait, arrived in this region. The earliest traces of human life so far discovered in these parts are the remains of mammoth-hunters in the Valley of Mexico, dating from 6000 B.C. or earlier. In this same region, originally an extensive lakeland plateau, signs of primitive civilizations of later date have been found. At all events, the first authenticated archaeological records date back to the second millennium B.C., when the archaic-ceramic cultures, which have been traced all over the area in question, flourished. At this stage maize, the staple crop of the ancient Central American civilizations, had long been cultivated by man, the population had become settled in many places, adept in the manufacture of ceramics and accustomed to burying with their dead offerings often of a rich nature.

Archaeology, in particular the discoveries of recent decades, has enabled us to reconstruct in broad outline a succession of civilizations which cover a period of some three thousand years, from the archaic-ceramic age to the end of the Aztec period. The general outlines and the duration of the different cultural phases can frequently be traced only through their art forms. In this connection it should be recalled that we have been left virtually no written records by the peoples and tribes connected with those civilizations and referring to their history. It was the Spanish conquerors and colonizers who first described the world they found there, and induced converted natives to record the customs and traditions of their people. Strangely enough, on the other hand, the cultural life which is so clearly visible in their works of art finds no parallel in surviving utensils of everyday life. The technology of the ancient civilizations of Central America never progressed beyond neolithic conditions. Metals such as copper and gold were not used until the late period and then only for ritual objects and ornaments. What is more, it is not even clear whether, and to what extent, the stone and bone implements typical of the archaic period were improved and developed in the course of time. It is a mystery how human beings with so scanty an equipment for promoting civilization were able to attain to such a high degree of culture. In this respect we are prevented from making the usual comparisons with the early civilizations of the Ancient World. Whereas in Egypt and Sumer we find the first metropolitan centres coming into existence during the transition from the Late Stone Age to the Bronze Age, when methods of production and social relationships underwent great changes, the evolution of the early Central American civilizations into no less imposing cultures appears to have taken place in different and rather special circumstances. To this day we lack any sort of closer insight into the social conditions which governed the lives of the ancient peoples of Central America, and are therefore still far from being able to determine what were the principal factors that influenced the development of their cultural life. We are still unable to account for their strange mixture of the primitive and the highly refined, as passively conservative and persistently progressive elements, for the rise of civilizations which flower with a tropical abundance only to fade again gradually from the moment of their unfolding.

Again and again we encounter basic differences as compared with the principal early cultures of the Ancient World. Thus, the great ancient civilizations of Central America grow up neither along a principal river system such as the Nile, the Mesopotamian rivers, the Indus and the Hoang-Ho, nor around an "inland sea" like the Mediterranean. They wax and wane in the uplands of the volcanic massif which runs through the territory they occupy, and in the tropical lowlands of its coastal areas, chiefly along the Atlantic seaboard. Always confined to the same area, determined for the most part by the configurations of the mountains, coastline and water-ways, they develop side by side with appreciable ramifications and in the main with a uniform rhythm. As is evident from the universal respect in which it was held, maize was their staple diet. Since stock-farming was totally unknown—the only domestic animals were a dog of hairless and fleshy breed and probably the turkey—hunting and fishing were, apart from agriculture, among their principal occupations. Cotton and vegetable fibres were used for weaving. In the upland areas where water was less abundant and which were more exposed to inclement weather, men appear from early times to have had recourse to artificial irrigation, terracing or ingenious devices such as the "floating gardens" on the lakes of the Valley of Mexico which so astounded the Spanish conquerors, in order to enhance their crops. The practice which is still encountered in many parts, of burning down undergrowth and jungle to win new land for cultivation, appears to date back to earliest times. Doubtless, important cultural zones such as the Valleys of Mexico, Cholula and Oaxaca, the central Gulf Coast and the territory inhabited by the Maya peoples were relatively thickly populated; and, in that they produced two crops per annum of maize, beans, sweet potatoes, pumpkins and peppers, whose cultivation, gathering and preparation require only a limited amount of labour, enough man-power would usually seem to have been available for building and enlarging the ceremonial metropolises. However, the sheer physical effort needed to produce the remarkable artistic creations of the ancient cultures of Central America is all the more astonishing when we remember that the builders of the countless temples and shrines, both large and small, had at their disposal neither metal implements nor pack- and draught-animals and were unfamiliar with the use of the wheel.

On the other hand, it should not be forgotten that the enormous output extending over many generations which we group together under the generic term "art of the ancient peoples of Central America" was basically intended for ritual purposes and thus made quite as many demands upon society as those activities which were directed towards ensuring the necessities of everyday living. For the survival of the community it was as important and as natural to invoke and appease the powerful forces in Nature—whether by means of magical rites or in observance of the dogmas of some religious creed—as to engage in husbandry, hunting and fishing. Indeed, primitive society undoubtedly regarded these rituals as the *sine quâ non* for the success of normal undertakings, as well as a means of warding off all manner of catastrophes. The fact that those who brought into being the old civilizations of Central America had to oppose Nature with what were by comparison extremely meagre resources leads us to conjecture that here ritual worship made greater calls upon the community's activities than it did, say, in ancient Egypt, Mesopotamia or China.

Not only do the evolution and growth of these civilizations remain matters for speculation, but also, in view of their geographical isolation, their origins too. Arising from this, we have the question as to their possible connection with early civilizations in other continents, which is suggested by the existence of related or outwardly similar art forms, architectonic and decorative motifs, resemblances between the racial types represented in ancient sculptures, or analogous ritual customs. Thus, a certain school of scientists in this field now tends to the opinion that cultural influences may have been derived, on the one hand from the Asian mainland, and from Oceania, on the other. But the main problem with which we are confronted is the fact that not a few of the parallel ritual and art forms first appear in epochs which show the ancient cultures of Central America already at the peak of their development, whereas the centres of culture outside the American continent which constitute possible points of contact had long availed themselves of material achievements which never found their way into the civilization-area of Central America. The same applies to other cultural zones of America, which for example had advanced further in the working of metals and the taming of domestic animals. Here, too, it is open to question to what extent active points of contact with such zones existed, above all with the ancient Andean cultures which continued to flourish over thousands of years in what is present-day Peru and which, in their way, disclose an evolutionary rhythm remarkably similar. During the course of what are in the archaeological sense observable times the area occupied by the ancient Central American civilizations seems at all events to have cut itself off like an island from the outside. And not only that—it slowly shrank in upon itself, the field of influence of the newly-developing cultures contracted. The Aztec civilization penetrated only a part of the area over which in earlier times the classic cultures of the ceremonial metropolises spread and flourished, whilst these in their turn covered a narrower territory than the preceding archaic-ceramic civilizations and their offshoots.

The particular development of the ancient civilizations of Central America can in fact be traced back to the archaic-ceramic cultures, those "mother cultures" which still have many customs in common with the Late Stone Age civilizations of other continents—such as the custom of tattooing, of dyeing the hair, the bodies of the dead and the burial implements with yellow ochre, secondary interment, the ritual of masks—and whose ceramic work shows forms and decorative designs of a kind similar to those of the archaic art of the Ohio and Mississippi area or the early Peruvian cultures. The archaic-ceramic cultures derive, so far as can be ascertained, from tribal communities which have settled down to husbandry, appear as relatively homogeneous socially, and whose ritual-artistic production does not exceed the scope of domestic handicraft. But already at an early stage such exceptionally abundant, varied and artistically refined pottery is made and used in burial-centres such as Tlatilco, that it is reasonable to assume that in those times social elites existed which became of paramount importance in subsequent cultures.

This opinion is supported by the likewise recent discovery of a highly-developed early culture, unmistakable traces of which—"cuckoo's eggs", so to speak, of genuine artistic quality—have since come to light also in archaic burial-areas such as Tlatilco and to which are also attributed the admirable monolithic sculptures unearthed in La Venta and other places all around the deepest indentation of the Gulf Coast. To this culture, now usually referred to as OLMEC, the origins of stone sculpture and monumental work, of hieroglyphic writing and the ritualistic calendar are attributed; that is to say, previously unknown artistic and intellectual forms of expression which subsequently predominated in the classic cultures. It is assumed that the unknown masters of the Olmec culture were in some ways connected with the beginnings of the new ritual which was ultimately superimposed upon the traditional community-cult of the archaic epoch and with whose advent a privileged caste of priests reaches a degree of prominence that extends its prerogatives to every social sphere. On the other hand, there has so far been no evidence of large-scale architecture or city-building within the orbit of Olmec culture, whose characteristic works of art and ritual objects have been traced all over the zone of early Central American civilization. The first large structures, made from earth-ramparts, air-dried bricks and rubble, date from the late archaic period, as does the pyramid of Cuicuilco on the outskirts of Mexico city. But there still remains the further transition to the planned grouping of large structures into town-like ceremonial centres. The classic cultures come into being where such metropolises are erected. In the highland valleys of Mexico (Teotihuacán) and Oaxaca (Monte Albán) this probably occurred already before historical times; in the Maya zone, several hundreds of years later.

At this turning-point new creative forces make their appearance, to an extent and a degree only conceivable as a consequence of radical changes in the social structure. The ceremonial cities which now come into being and are frequently enlarged in the course of generations, constitute the hubs of a wonderful activity, which testifies to the existence of powerful social forces directing the collective endeavours. In the large ritual centres, with their monumental architecture, we have evidence of a desire at this stage to create imposing works, as well as of a tendency towards magnificence, alike in the ornamentation of ceremonial buildings and in many other manifestations of ritual worship. Now for the first time we find artistic representa-tions of rulers and dignitaries, mostly in direct association with the depiction of sacred or ceremonial activities. The "Old Empire" of the Maya offers the most numerous and clear-cut examples. Gorgeous raiment, fantastic head-gear, rich jewellery and ornaments, staffs of office and sceptre-like emblems attest to power and rank. In the murals and vase-paintings which are sometimes found to deviate into the anecdotal, we see grand seigneurs with large retinues, surrounded by the most various signs of what is clearly temporal luxury. But even in these instances the bounds of ceremonial usage are not overstepped; we find no parallel to the scenes from everyday and private life which have come down to us from other ancient civilizations and which are so informative for the study of cultural history. Those masters who are always portrayed in anonymous inaccessibility were doubtless the rulers of those times, the controllers of the collective forces out of whose co-operation came forth the most brilliant ancient cultures of America. If they were dynastic rulers, how can we account for the fact that there is not the remotest allusion to their personalities, or for the fact that to this day no trace of court life is to be found? Nor does tradition suggest anything of the kind. Here, too, we have to fall back on conjecture, and we are led to suppose a theocratic system, in which priestly castes exercise spiritual as well as temporal power, and which reflects the culture of the "Old Empire" of the Maya in the richest and materially most luxurious, the upland culture of Monte Albán and Teotihuacán in a more puritanical and militant form.

Each one of these classic cultures evolves specific traits in its ritual, its art and its customs; the various peoples of the classic period, though, are more clearly marked off from one another; besides the Maya, there are the Totonacs of the Gulf Coast, the Zapotecs in the region of Monte Albán and the still unnamed people of Teotihuacán. The origins of these tribes are shrouded in darkness; their history is practically unknown, as are also their mutual relationships, though the distribution of objects from one zone over other regions testifies to some such contact. For centuries the various classic cultures existed side by side, even though the upland cultures probably originated earlier and had perhaps already passed their zenith while the diffusion of the classic civilizations along the Gulf Coast and in the Maya zone was still actively proceeding. The highland cultures occupied a territory which appears to have been more limited geographically and less rich in natural resources, though their organization was obviously more rigid and their urge to expand more pronounced. Amongst them no sign of several rival ceremonial cities is to be discovered; they seem, rather, to have established "colonies" in distant parts, as is evidenced in particular by the Teotihuacán culture, traces of which have been encountered over a wide area reaching as far as present-day Guatemala.

During the "Old Empire" epoch there was a veritable "founding fever" in the MAYA ZONE, when large and small ritual centres sprang up, principally in the fertile river and lake region which forms a semicircle around the foot of the Yucatán peninsula, and then in Yucatán itself. Thanks to the mathematical genius of the Maya of the classic period, whose supreme achievement was the institution of a sacred calendar by which they regulated their entire religious life; thanks to their practice of periodically erecting memorial steles in their ritual

centres, inscribed with glyph series giving the dedicatory date, we are able, with the aid of the deciphered Mayan calendar, to follow the progressive stages of development of the "Old Empire". The oldest discovered memorial stele of this kind, in Uaxactún (Guatemala), bears a date which corresponds to the year 328 by our reckoning; in the same way numerous important ritual centres of the ensuing two hundred years emerge, among them Tikal, Piedras Negras (Guatemala), Copán (Honduras), Palenque and Yaxchilán. The next two centuries, the seventh and eighth by our reckoning, count as the golden age of the "Old Empire", which passes over into a period of rapid decline, fading out altogether in the year 889. In a like manner we can now ascertain when it was that most of these centres reached the peak of their development, and thereby "place" their relevant architectural and artistic achievements; this presents us with the picture of a flame of concentrated creative genius leaping from ritual centre to ritual centre, which after burning itself out in one place, is kindled again in another and finally, after a final mighty upsurge, suddenly dies out.

Towards the end of the ninth century all traces of the classic cultures disappear. No reasons have so far been found for this simultaneous disappearance of the most splendid ancient civilizations of the American continent. The collapse of the classic upland cultures is probably connected with the invasion by warlike barbarian tribes from the north. The cities of the "Old Empire" of the Maya seem simply to have been deserted and abandoned to the jungle, perhaps as a result of a general exhaustion of the productive forces of society and an inability on the part of a ruling priestly caste which had grown unpopular to check the progressive decay. In general, then, it would seem that an alternation of internal decline with pressure from barbarian invaders, which we know from history to have been fatal to other ancient civilizations, brought also the classic cultures of ancient Mexico to an end.

During the second half of the tenth century a new phase in the cultural history of the Central American region begins, a period which is partly illuminated historically by traditional records from a later time. From now on, the Mexican central plateau becomes the focal point of activity. True, the crests of the first fresh wave of civilization since the decay of the classic cultures are widely separated in space: they are represented by the cities of Tula on the Mexican high plateau and those of Chichén Itzá in northern Yucatán. But archaeology has meanwhile also shown that Tula, the legendary capital of the Toltec peoples, and Chichén Itzá belong to the same cultural orbit, in which the mythical Toltec ruler "Superbly-plumed Snake"—Quetzalcoatl in the spreading Nahua tongue, Kukulcán in Mayan language—plays a significant part, raised by tradition to superhuman level. It is not yet known whether the Toltecs came with the first conquerors who settled in the region of the classic cultures and who were there doubtless lastingly influenced by the latter. At all events, not only are the first new cultural achievements, to which the erection of new cities testify, associated with their names and traces, but also the first attempts at a hitherto unknown regimen, instituted by predominant warlike groups, headed by chieftains avid for worldly power who seek to extend their dominion over vast territories. At about the same time in Yucatán the Maya culture achieves a new lease of life which conforms to the prevailing type of dynastically ruled city state, whose overlords like the mighty Itzás of Chichén go in for Mexican customs and culture. Similar trends are found also among the Mixtecs, who now dominate the Valley of Oaxaca and spread across the area of the ancient ritual centre of Cholula in the direction of the Valley of Mexico. However, Toltec rule soon yielded to the invasion of fresh conquering hordes, who proceeded to set up their own small dominions in the Valley of Mexico and thence to extend their influence over a wider area. In the "New Empire" of the Maya of Yucatán the cultural renascence lasts until the close of the twelfth century; after the fall of Chichén Itzá, however, it goes under ingloriously during the protracted local wars between the various city rulers.

During this period of general unrest the impulse for conquest on the part of the Nahuatl peoples who have penetrated into the Mexican high plateau operates as a constant factor. The Aztec race is a late arrival among them. Legend has it that the Aztecs, who migrated from the north, were exiled to a wild island in the Texcoco Lake by the chieftains of the tribes which had by then settled in the Valley of Mexico. There they found the city of Tenochtitlán in 1325 and proceed to work with unfailing vigour and determination towards subjugating their neighbours. By the second half of the fifteenth century the Aztec rulers have become the lords and monarchs of the principalities of the Valley of Mexico; they then make use of their new powers in order, by means of successful wars of aggression coupled with a cunning policy of subjugation, to build up the first and only great empire in the early history of Central America. At the turn of the fifteenth century the Aztec empire is at its zenith. Whether or not the reign of Moctezuma II (1502–20), the opening years of which were dogged by harvest failures and pestilences, sowed the seeds of definitive internal decay, we have no means of telling; but the fact remains that the general turmoil within the Aztec empire at the time opened the way to the Spaniards, who advanced to the very gates of Tenochtitlán. And with the breaking apart of Aztec power the whole civilization of old Mexico comes to an abrupt end.

The power and glory of ancient Mexico had had one last flowering, but concentrated as never before in one single spot: the city of TENOCHTITLÁN. The descriptions of the Spaniards, who were fascinated by the size and splendour of the city, at the same time betray how far the division into social strata had been carried, within the framework of the basic conditions imposed upon the ancient civilizations of Central America. In state and society there was, besides the priesthood which monopolized ritual and ideological matters, a powerful class which derived its privileges from its military, political and economic status, while the common people had to bear the weight of both. Furthermore, the Aztec rulers exacted high tribute from allied townships, vassals and subject peoples. Significantly enough, after theological-didactic treatises, tribute lists occupy the most important place among the Aztec written records that have come down to us; they give detailed accounts of the commodity payments rendered to the state and court treasuries. Tremendous wealth flowed into the capital, where the palaces of the Aztec princes arose beside the towering temples, on whose markets were to be found the products of the widespread regions of the empire and which had become the centre of artisan-ship in a variety of specialized trades. The working of copper, gold and silver seems to have been on a fairly large scale, though still confined to ritual and luxury articles; as valuables, however, brightly-coloured stones, above all jade and latterly turquoise too, were preferred to the rare metals. Cocoa-beans were the medium of exchange used for an incipient barter trade. In contrast to a manifestly progressive improvement in material welfare and social conditions, a rigid state religion based on dark superstition prevailed in the ritual and intellectual sphere. Attempts at reform in this field undertaken towards the end of the fifteenth century in Texcoco, a neighbouring town at this time rivalling Tenochtitlán in importance, seem to have been suppressed again after Aztec supremacy had been firmly established. In its sculpture alone the last Aztec period is animated by a new creative zeal outstripping traditional norms.

Into the orbit of the ancient civilizations of Mexico which disappear with the collapse of the Aztec empire came also marginal areas which must have maintained an independent existence since early times, areas where the classic cultures had never gained a lasting foothold and where a simpler and apparently less rigid way of life persisted. That applies above all to the territories of Colima, Nayarit and Jalisco on the Pacific side of Central Mexico, whose terra-cottas are of particular interest since they afford us unique evidence of the everyday life of people in those times. We may regard this zone, which preserved its independence also during the Aztec period, as "the land of the Phaeacians" of ancient Mexico.

This book on the ancient art of Mexico does not take into account the southern marginal cultures of what is present-day Guatemala and El Salvador, mostly variations of the archaic and classic cultures here dealt with. The area over which the old Central American civilization extended does not correspond with present-day political boundaries. Nevertheless, with the exception of the southerly zone of the classic Maya culture and its predecessors, modern Mexico —which is now classed politico-geographically as a part of the North American continent— includes within its boundaries all the important cultural areas known to us that archaeology counts among the old civilizations of Central America. For this reason we feel justified in restricting ourselves to the early art of Mexico. For the same reason we do not here concern ourselves with the early art of north-western Mexico (Casas Grandes), since its points of refer-ence lead preponderantly to the art of New Mexico and Arizona, which belong to the orbit of the ancient North American cultures.

*

A great deal, including countless specimens, of the ancient art of Mexico must be regarded as irretrievably lost. The Spanish conquerors in the first place seized everything that they

regarded as precious, and then went on to destroy systematically those things that were associated with the ancient indigenous cults. Of the show-pieces sent to Europe at this time, the
goldsmiths' work which Albrecht Dürer so admired in the Netherlands, the feather work and
the mosaics made from precious stones, only a few unique specimens exist today; likewise
various folding books painted on animal skins or paper made from tree bark. On the other
hand, the soil and climate of Mexico claimed everything made from perishable or delicate
materials: textiles, lacquer- and paper-work, plaited and feather-covered fabrics of every kind.
Few murals and wood carvings survived. But the Mexican soil harbours virtually inexhaustible quantities of artifacts of stone or baked clay, together with objects made from bone, shell,
copper and gold, which have withstood the ravages of time. Again and again archaeologically
important pieces and peerless works of art are unearthed by persons tilling or digging the soil,
though many of these continue to be destroyed by those who know no better. As yet, only a
fraction of the buried ruins and other archaeological sites so far discovered has been systematically explored; nevertheless, such explorations have, particularly during the past twenty-five
years, caused us to change our views appreciably on the old civilizations of Mexico and their
art. Thus, quite a large proportion of the works of art reproduced in this volume consists of new
finds and examples of the artistic achievement of cultures whose existence has only recently
been established or whose importance is now increasingly recognized.

Practically all the old Mexican works of art were essentially ritual or cultic in character.
Sacred buildings, such as temples and shrines, the walled courtyards devoted to ritual ball-games
and the groups of edifices resembling palaces and monasteries, which form part of the structure
of the ceremonial cities, lend the architecture its characteristic stamp. Monumental sculpture,
stucco and mural work develop during the classic period in combination with the architecture.
Stone carvings often, and clay ceremonial vessels or figurines nearly always, form part of the
grave offerings connected with funeral rites.

All such coherent information as we possess concerning religion and ritual in ancient
Mexico derives from records dating back to the beginnings of Spanish colonial rule and so
concerns chiefly the official Aztec religion, with its pantheistic and blood-thirsty cult: a
theological system which may be regarded as a probably somewhat coarsened and brutalized
version of the fundamental notions common to the old Central American religions as to the
nature of the universe and the relationship within it between man and the supernatural powers.
It is a theology which rests on a conception of the universe as being ruled by fearful deities
representing the constellations and the forces of nature, who are engaged in an unceasing and
merciless struggle, a struggle perpetuating an incalculable chain of cosmic catastrophes in
which worlds are destroyed and recreated. It is the inexorable fate of all existing things to be
subject to these gods, who inhabit the four cardinal points and the centre of the earth, and whom
it is as impossible to evade as it is for mortals to influence the planets in their courses or to stay

the forces of nature. The welfare or ill-fortune of mankind is of little consequence to the great gods. The fate of peoples hangs upon whether well- or ill-intentioned superhuman powers gain the upper hand, and the inhabitants of earth, caught as it were in an inescapable trap, can survive only so long as the priests, whose eyes are perpetually on the precipitous abode of the gods, succeed in procuring a respite, meted out day by day and aeon by aeon, by dint of ceaseless sacrifices and entreaties.

The price the gods exacted consisted above all of human blood and of hearts torn from the bodies of the destined victims, a sacrificial cult represented in the art of the classic period, and which, it is said, the Toltec ruler Quetzalcoatl, whom legend endows with promethean attributes, vainly sought to redeem by proffering snakes and butterflies. Whilst the Toltecs and Aztecs carried the ritual of bloody sacrifice to extremes, they safeguarded the interests of the State, in that they saw to it that not the able-bodied men of their own race, but prisoners who were taken during campaigns specially conducted for this purpose, were sacrificed.

From the Toltec epoch onwards the horrible aspects of this ritual are also clearly reflected in art, which often takes on a macabre character. Skulls constitute a very frequent decorative motif, altars and temples become sculpted charnel-houses, gods are represented by terrible symbols of destruction (plates 93, 94, IV). But it would be a mistake to see in this crass manifestation of a barbaric cult—the more striking, the greater the artistic refinement with which it is represented—the only typical feature of Aztec art. Besides the sculptures engendered by a gruesome state ritual, we find, especially in the sculpture of the late Aztec period, works of vital and unforced naturalness such as are not encountered elsewhere among the stone carvings of old Mexico (plates 95, 98, 101). Partaking of a conception according to which the cosmic order is maintained only by virtue of perpetual sacrifices, where the sun must be fed with human hearts and the maize brought to germination by human blood, an art which is given over to macabre symbolism acquires the significance of a symbolic sacrificial rite. For the sacred images are not for the edification of man, but intended for the eye of the gods; they seek the favour of the terrible powers which can be assuaged and warded off only by incessant adequate sacrifices.

For sheer immoderation, at all events, the Aztec cult of sacrifice is hard to beat. Excessive, too, is the number of gods worshipped in the Aztec religion, as well as the number of actual and symbolic attributes with which they are as a rule simultaneously endowed. In this respect, too, the Aztecs seem to have been prone to accept more or less uncritically whatever their various more civilized neighbours had to offer. They appear to have had very little inclination for speculative thought; their calendric system is virtually the most primitive that is to be found among the ancient peoples of Mexico.

Of the ancient peoples of Mexico, it was the MAYA of the "Old Empire" who attained the highest degree of theological and speculative thinking; their calendric system counts among the most unique and remarkable intellectual achievements of early human history. In their ritual thinking the Maya were positively obsessed by time and the rotation of the heavenly bodies, by the never-ending sequence of days and periods to be counted up, co-ordinated, and noted down by means of pictorial and glyphic signs, which, as far as they have been deciphered, can be shown to celebrate the passage of time always anew in inexhaustible permutations. The pictorial signs in a calligraphically elegant relief-style rich in nuances (plates 47, 48) are one of the hall-marks of Mayan art which—in contradistinction to, say, the inscribed Egyptian or Assyrian relief sculptures—weaves figures with sculpted inscriptions into a well-balanced organic whole.

Concerning the religious conceptions and liturgical usages of the classic cultures we know for the most part just so much as can be deduced from their art. The unsurpassed activity in all fields of sacred architecture and art points to the fact that during that period religious cults and theological zeal reached a peak. Deriving as they do from a common root-conception and set within the framework of a ritual that is in broad outline common to all, each one of the classic cultures yet bears its own individual stamp and so also gives rise to its own style in architecture and sculpture, exhibits specific ritual objects peculiar to it, and is in art, too, devoted to certain favoured gods. In the case of the Maya it was, apparently, above all the god of the sun or of the planetal order, in Teotihuacán the god of rain or of the moist elements, who later figured in the Aztec pantheon under the name of Tlaloc. To identify the various gods offers a difficulty also for the reason that they are not actually portrayed but shown symbolically. Portraits of gods, such as we associate with the art of the Ancient World, are strictly speaking not encountered. Everything that expresses any relationship with the divine is transfigured and disguised; abstract symbols, particular emblems and symbolic attributes, animal tokens harking back to totemic conceptions and symbolic masks all serve the purpose of representational imagery. In the case of the Rain God worshipped in Teotihuacán we have, for instance: billowy lines, drops of water, balls of cloud, marine shells, plumed jaguars or serpents and finally the mask of the divinity with spectacle-like rims around the eyes, symbolic perhaps of clouds, and a mouth formed like the jaws of a jaguar with threatening fangs (plate 24).

Among all the symbolic representations the MASK, which embodies two-fold magical powers, ranks first; *pars pro toto*, it conjures up into the face it frames the whole being symbolized by it, and transmits to the wearer the power concentrated in the mask-face, transforming him into its ally and partner. The age-old conception of the magic power of the mask lives on in the ancient cultures of Mexico, which in their art take up this motif in the most diverse forms, varying from imitations modelled in clay of masks worn for ritual purposes, through small amulets and monumental stone carvings, to gigantic masks adorning buildings, such as are to be found in Uaxactún on the oldest Mayan pyramid known to us, or those that constitute the structural element of whole façades in the architecture of the "New Empire" of the Maya of

Yucatán. Were one to look for a single favourite theme as representative of the art of the ancient peoples of Mexico, it would above all be the mask motif. In the archaic-ceramic cultures we find an unsophisticated mask still predominating, showing a human or animal face with realistic features uncomplicated even where the mask is split up into two visually heterogeneous but sculpturally equivalent halves symbolizing dualistic conceptions (plate 8). In Olmec art we encounter for the first time those noble stone masks sublimating the human face by rendering its purest plastic grandeur without any supplementary adornment (plate 9), a type of mask which receives its classic shape at the hands of the sculptors of the Teotihuacán period (plates 25, 26) and which is encountered later also in the art of the Nahuatl peoples (plate 102).

Also derived from Olmec art is the daemonic mask, that fantastic synthesis of realistic yet—where the terrible or grotesque is introduced—transfigured forms in which human and animal features are frequently mingled. The Olmec prototype of this mask, deriving from the fearsome features of the jaguar, the animal representing the all-devouring elemental powers, recalls the Gorgon faces of Greek archaic art, except that the effect of paralysing terror, which is mirrored there, appears to be heightened by bold harmony of design (plate I).

The ritualistic functions of the mask are evidenced by the many works of art of the classic cultures which represent masked persons or show masks as appurtenances of ceremonial costume, of head-gear or of priestly robes. In other instances masks are used as a fantastic frame for the head and in that way hark back to what is perhaps their original function, the disguising of the whole body. It was not only for ritual purposes that magic costumes of feathers and animal skins were worn; in the battle-scene from the frescoes of Bonampák the Mayan fighters of the classic period are clad in symbolic outfits of this nature, which were later to become the customary garb of the Toltec and Aztec warrior orders, the Eagle and Tiger formations.

Masks and disguises, as well as tattooing and the deformation of certain parts of the body, feature already in the ritual usages of the ARCHAIC-CERAMIC PERIOD. These customs, as well as those connected with archaic burial rites whereby the dead were interred with grave offerings such as vessels, stone and bone implements and, above all, ceramic figurines, are transmitted from this period to later cultures. The ceramic figurines consist in the main of small female statuettes often no more than three or four inches long, usually naked though tattooed in bright colours, always with carefully elaborated head-dress, sometimes carrying a child, a dog or a bird, sometimes in a dancing attitude or also with a double face or head. Among the male figures, recognizable by their loin-cloths, those with helmet-like or other distinctive head-gear represent dancers or acrobats; others appear attired for the ritual ball-game (plates 1-7). Frequently statuettes of hunchbacks and other misshapen beings are encountered, which probably derive from taboo-ideas, whilst the numerous representations of animals in the shape of vessels, whistles and clay rattles or upon roller-stamps are likely to be connected with totemistic notions. The archaic terra-cottas, though they already follow clearly established norms of presentation and style, display a freshness and a sensuous spontaneity, which in the later but by all standards still archaic ceramics of Colima, Nayarit and Jalisco, sometimes assume a touch of the burlesque (plates 67, 68, 74). Without doubt, the potters of Tlatilco and Colima adopted a similar attitude towards their work as did the sculptors of Palenque and Tula: it is always invested with a ritual significance. It is evident that in this respect the standards that applied at the time of the archaic-ceramic cultures were different from those of later periods, when a monumental and ceremonial art held the field. Archaic art reflects a ritualistic life still cut to the pattern of a democratic order of tribal communities, and not yet a religious system functionally and ideologically controlled by a privileged priestly caste. True, there are already signs that deities were then worshipped whom we encounter again in priest-led religions of a later period, as for example the gods of fire and of wind; but the simplicity of the archaic masks and statuettes which point in this direction differentiates them clearly from the theologically interpreted works of art of ensuing cultures. Reduced to simplest terms, archaic art can be said to be the expression of a popular cult on which priest-led religions are at later stages super-imposed, these in turn putting their stamp upon art. It would be interesting to follow this comparison further and show how elements pertaining rather to the genuine imaginative world of folk-ritual break through again and again in an art dominated by priest-led religions. In this connection it should be emphasized that the schematic lines of demarcation that archae-ology has to draw between successively developing cultures in no way denotes that one ends where the other begins. We shall probably obtain a truer picture if we imagine the ceremonial metropolises which determined the ritual and art of their time as islands of civilization in much more primitive "archaic" surroundings, economically dependent upon these and only secure as long as the ruling priestly castes retained their prerogatives there. If, as is to be assumed, these castes maintained their rule primarily by ideological means, then the priest-led religion and its ritual had to be made to prevail over the primitive popular cults wherever they persisted, including the production of ritualistic artifacts. Whilst architecture, stone carvings and painting by their very nature constituted the art of the ceremonial metropolises, clay modelling was familiar to everybody from early times. What more natural than that the priestly castes should bring clay modelling for ritual purposes also under their control?

Hitherto, the modelling of ceramic figures, too, had always been unhindered; within the limits of the generally respected norms, the modeller was left to his own devices and allowed to exercise his creative initiative and skill. But now a significant change takes place with the development of the CLASSIC CULTURES: moulds are introduced, with whose help not only small terra-cottas but also large-scale and compound clay sculptures could be moulded, an art which grows increasingly effective. Henceforth, the type of presentation and degree of elaboration correspond exactly to the norms set by the moulds, which are also made of baked

18

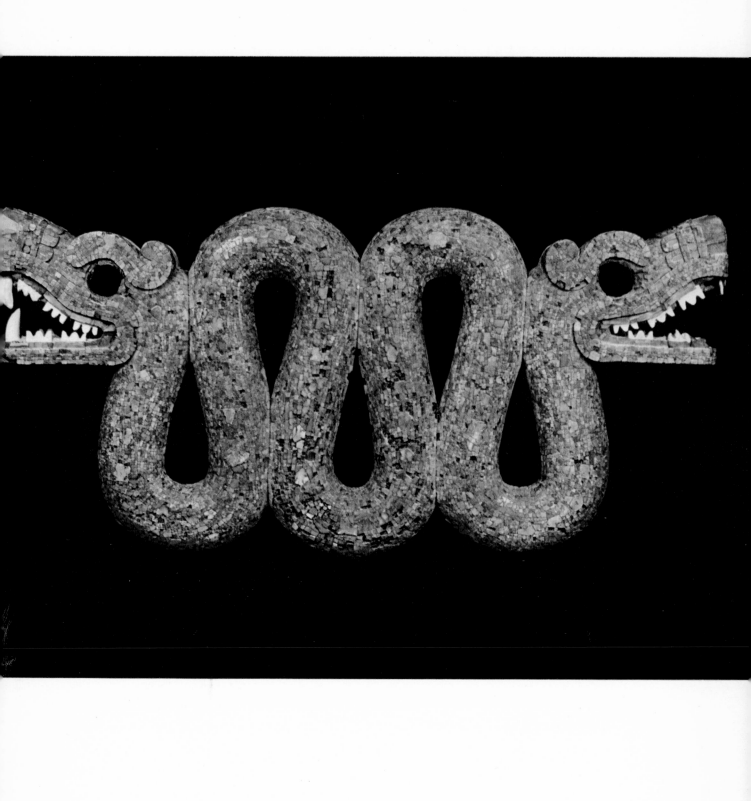

clay. So remarkable is this transition to new, mechanical methods of production in the techno-logically conservative old civilizations of Mexico, that we must ask ourselves to what extent practical considerations can be held responsible. The most likely explanation seems to us to be that this departure was above all dictated by a desire to make the most popular branch of creative ritual art likewise subject to the norms of a priest-led religion. In point of fact the mould-made ceramics are seen to follow the general tendencies of the ritual art of the ceremonial cities. In place of the now simple, now bolder, sensibility of the hand-made terra-cottas we find a pretentious formalism, resulting from the tendency, characteristic of classic art, to present symbolic ornamental designs and motifs so prominently that they everywhere catch the eye. Unquestionably a loss of direct artistic expression is to some extent balanced by a greater degree of accomplishment, in so far as the moulds now make it possible to transmit the mature style of classical art also to clay sculpture. Many of the finest works of figure pottery were created in this way. But, in general, the more classic art is given over to formalism, the more evi-dent does the decline in artistic quality of moulded clay sculpture become. Through excess of ornamentation ceramic work ultimately comes to reflect the esoteric utterances of cere-monial cults.

The introduction of pre-manufactured moulds for the ritual pottery of the classic period also indicates, however, that art ruled by the priestly castes had outgrown the imagination of the common people. With its esoteric symbolism and its complicated pomp, ritual art now served a religion intelligible only to a few privileged initiates, and this was precisely its function. For it was not intended to appeal to human beings, from whom, indeed, it frequently remained hidden. It should be recalled that the tomb figures were interred with the dead, offerings were buried in the earth, monuments frequently had their undersides—which were hidden from view—richly sculpted, while gloomy temple chambers accessible only to the priests were lavishly decorated with reliefs and paintings. The aim of ritual art in old Mexico was always to conjure the higher powers. In the archaic terra-cottas of dancers and acrobats (plate 1), the reliefs of Maya priests absorbed in ritual worship (plate 49), the Aztec sculptures of the servants of the god Xipe wearing the skin of the sacrificed (plate 95), precisely the same basic idea is expressed in successive ages and cultures: to give visual expression to a veneration for the powers that govern matters of life and death. Nor, in the old civilizations of Mexico, is ritual art meant for human edification by creating anthropomorphic images of deities or by erecting sacred buildings inviting a foregathering of men. It is intended only to capture the eye of the gods, to "afford them pleasure" in the form of works and images which provide evidence of man's ritual devotion to the higher powers. In this connection, realism and accuracy of visual rendering had a magical significance; nothing that was fashioned for this purpose was allowed to have its direct impact impaired. So, in this matter of representational art, men always came back to themselves, objectified themselves in it, zealously reproduced their own characteristic features, portrayed themselves with the utmost meticulousness in ritual garb—and so unconsciously erected their own memorial, whose value and significance we have now begun to appreciate and so more fully understand.

*

The plates in this volume have been so arranged as to illustrate the art of old Mexico by monuments and sculptures in which the style of the most important periods and cultures so far brought to light is given fullest and purest expression. Nowadays not only do we distinguish periods and cultures according to their particular artistic style, which frequently serves as a virtual archaeological passport, but we are able to discern the phases and periods when art seems to have been at its best; we are thus in a position to exemplify the archaeological and historico-stylistic connections in works that bear the stamp of great art. Admittedly, a selection of pictures based on such standards remains one-sided and to some extent incomplete, above all if it leaves out of account significant and characteristic variations of a given style, which we consider was no longer at, or had not yet reached the level of a particular culture's mature art. But recent research and observation have made this kind of selection possible; we hope, nevertheless, that new finds and further investigation will before long render ours obsolete.

The ancient art of Mexico, unlike that of Egypt, does not carry the stamp of one basic style cast from a single mould and practically unaffected by the passage of time and changing events. Its style shows a continuity over some three thousand years, but with continually new variations of certain underlying forms and modes of expression, often developing along parallel lines; in pottery, stone carving and architecture these are already encountered in the earliest works with which we are now familiar, whereas in those that follow they are not simply copied in the conventional manner, but expressly modified from epoch to epoch and from culture to culture.

The beginnings of great ARCHITECTURE date back to the late archaic period. The archaic round pyramid of Cuicuilco, previously referred to, shows the characteristic form of this kind of old Mexican sacred building, that bulkiness of structure diminishing step by step towards the top. Pyramids are mostly built on a rectangular, frequently on a square ground-plan, have sharp-edged profiles, rising by steps or irregularly graded slopes, whilst the monumental stairway leading to the sanctuary which crowns the buildings on the side exposed to view, accentuates the steepness of the building (plates 23, 44, 57, 91).

Only in name do the Mexican pyramids correspond with their Egyptian counterparts; they are not tombs. Nor are they, like the ziggurats of the old Mesopotamian civilizations, the crowning structure of an enclosed city nucleus. Here the pyramid serves as the sloping substructure of temples, is the principal and most striking element of a sacred large-scale architecture wholly devoted to creating the most telling outward effect. As a rule the sacred centres extend over a wide area, which sometimes, as in Monte Albán or Xochicalco, was gained by artificially levelling a hill-side; by means of platforms of varying heights, graduated terraces and open courts surrounded by massive structures, the effect of depth and spaciousness is still more magnificently conveyed, the idea of height by the recession of the rising walls and by mounting stairways (plate 36). The eye rests always on a maximum surface area. Pyramids of varying sizes are spread over the ceremonial precincts, in some cases in irregular groups, in others arranged symmetrically. Where the cities of the "Old Empire" of the Maya are concerned, the main emphasis is on the vertical components, in the case of the highland cultures the horizontally graduated aspect is stressed.

In the Maya area a few temples erected upon pyramids have remained nearly intact; otherwise we have to rely on sculptured and pictorial representations of such shrines. They are for the most part rectangular, windowless structures crowned by an ornamented roof-crest running along the front side, with smooth walls broken only on the façade by doorways leading into the interior (plate 43). The interior is decidedly cramped for space. The Maya of the "Old Empire" used the false arch with which to span their chambers, and so achieved room-breadths of barely twelve feet, usually still less; hence the inner rooms of their buildings are virtually galleries whose width does not greatly exceed the thickness of the walls. Elsewhere the buildings were roofed over with beams; this leads, particularly in the later cultures, to the use of pillars and pilasters as supports—also employed in the architecture of the "New Empire" of the Maya in Yucatán (plate 80).

The other ceremonial buildings were erected in a similar manner; they usually rise from artificial terraces and are often grouped around inner courtyards. Already in the classic cultures we encounter those complex buildings now known as "palaces", characteristic of the architecture of the Maya of Yucatán (plate 81). The outside architecture which is turned to the open and the sunlight is invariably grand and noble, while the inner aspect is gloomy, narrow and uncomfortable. During the late phase there are signs of an attempt to provide larger and lighter inner chambers. Of the palaces of the nobles dating from the Aztec period scarcely a trace is any longer to be found; but from all we have learned of them, these secular buildings made allowances for the practical requirements of their occupants.

Much zeal and architectonic skill were lavished upon the construction of the courts devoted to the sacred ball-game. Other edifices which have been discovered in various ceremonial cities, and whose function can be surmised from their construction, are the so-called observatories. The three-storeyed tower situated in one of the courtyards of the "Palacio" of Palenque is believed to have been used for observing the heavens by the priests of this metropolis, which, in the seventh century, was a centre of Mayan astrological ritual. The Mayan architects attempted to erect also structures of several floors, stepping back each superposed storey. Thanks to the abundant supply of limestone they were able to construct their buildings out of massive blocks or small stone slabs and mortar, and to lend them greater stability than were the builders of the upland cultures, who used sun-dried bricks and rubble mixed with mortar—one of the reasons the Maya buildings have for the most part lasted better.

The little attention that was paid to the planning of the inside architecture finds its counterpart in the sparseness of sepulchral fashioning. Despite the considerable role that burial ritual played, properly designed tombs are rare; the exception is Monte Albán, where grave-chambers dressed with stone are numerous, a tradition which is carried further in the grave-pits of Mitla with their elaborately sculpted inner walls.

Opening on to wide vistas and the untrammelled light of day, the ritual architecture of the classic and later period calls for the complementary effect of sculpture and painting, for which purpose it offers large and clearly ordered outer surfaces. In many instances the whole structure was covered with stucco and given a coating of colour. The coloured stucco-reliefs which covered the outer walls of the buildings at Palenque may even have excelled in richness and elegance the decoration of the inner chamber. The fragments of murals unearthed at Teotihuacán suggest that a number of buildings were originally adorned with frescoes. Nowadays we can only conjecture the glorious sight the cities of the classical period must have presented in their own day.

The sculptural decoration of sacred structures during the classical period varies from culture to culture. The Maya frequently carved the lintels of the temple doorways and the steps and curbs of monumental open stairways; in Teotihuacán the outer walls of the late "Quetzalcoatl" pyramid were thus adorned (plate 24), while the art of the Tajin culture, given—as is mentioned below—particularly to sophisticated stone carvings, excels them all. The chiselled stone dressing of the famous niche-pyramid of the Tajin (plate 57) recalls early Chinese art, and the recently discovered remnants of the temple that stood upon it are truly magnificent examples of the lavishly ornamented carvings of the classic Tajin style. Later, there is the strikingly sculptural impact of the architecture of the Toltec period, with its massively carved door-posts and caryatids, its stone pilasters adorned with reliefs, and the carved friezes running the length of the walls. The massive style of the Mexican highlands, developed to its highest pitch of monumental splendour in Tula (plate 76), has its counterpart in the somewhat less rigid Maya-Toltec architecture of Chichén Itzá (plate 80). Also in the north of Yucatán, the so-called Puuc style shows a different trend: it develops certain baroque tendencies prevailing in the preceding phase of Maya art and by now covering the façades with stone filigree-work, cluttering the plain walls with decorative motifs, thus converting the sacred buildings into pretentious shrines, which call to mind the buildings of south-eastern India and the Khmers (plates 84, 85). In Mitla, in the upland valley of Oaxaca, the adornment of the main structure with carved panels—an art which at this period had apparently become fashionable—was carried out in yet another manner (plates 86, 87). Finally, during the Aztec period the austere sobriety of their sacred architecture limits the amount of sculptural embellishment, confined henceforth principally to stone pegs projecting from the walls of pyramids and carved in the shapes of snakes or skulls, and to sculpted snakes mounted on the basements and stairways (plate 92).

Large-scale architecture and monumental stone sculpture apparently also sprang from various roots in ancient Mexico. Stone sculpture, appearing only in a rudimentary and coarse form in the archaic-ceramic cultures, all at once becomes, within the orbit of the Olmec culture—of which, so far at least, no traces of large-scale architecture are known—something like an artistic phenomenon. The Olmecs must have been born sculptors. With a self-assurance not otherwise encountered during initial phases of artistic development and an extraordinarily marked sensibility for style, they created sculptural works, each of which was a masterpiece of its kind, whether they take the form of jade figurines a few inches high or enormous mono-lithic carvings in basalt like the colossal heads and altars of La Venta (plates 12–14, 17–19, 21, I). Olmec sculptures are recognizable at a glance, as much by their outward stylistic traits —the compelling heads and profiles with full-lipped trapezial mouth, fleshily soft features, artificially deformed oblong craniums, designs which frequently pass over into jaguar motifs, an ornamentation entailing incised curved lines—as by the masterly carving and finish, by the smoothly rounded, swelling and gleaming polished surfaces. Sometimes statuesquely poised, sometimes dramatically alive, the Olmec sculptures display a realistic simplicity of form so refined that it achieves without effort what in our opinion is the fullest artistic effect. Symbolic-decorative and similar details in themselves of little sculptural merit, which in the statuary of later cultures often have so many flourishes that they destroy the main outlines, are in Olmec sculpture mostly wrought as delicate relief and engraving work; whatever may have been its actual purpose, the effect is certainly to leave the plastic values unimpaired. In every kind of stone carving, as practised in old Mexico, the Olmecs have shown themselves to be masters whose work has seldom been surpassed: they made large and small carved figures, altars, reliefs, masks and an enormous variety of little symbolic objects, and they worked porous and hard types of stone with equal facility.

The cultures of the classic period by no means all engaged in STONE CARVING to an equal extent. The civilization of Monte Albán seems to have been least productive in this field. The most outstanding sculptures found within this orbit, the reliefs of the so-called "Danzantes" (plate 33) date from a very early, probably pre-Zapotec epoch. From the great period of Monte Albán we have up to this day discovered nothing more than fragments of relief carvings, and no large-scale sculptures of note. Very different is the case of Teotihuacán, whose wonderful stone masks are among the most impressive creations of ancient Mexican sculpture (plates 25, 26), and which produced also a particularly massive style in statuary which follows the con-tours of the original stone block (plate 31). The emphasis on flat surfaces and on horizontal lines peculiar to the art of Teotihuacán lends a stark, solemn immobility to its stone carvings, meant for viewing head-on (plate 27). By way of contrast, we have the sculpture of the Maya and of the Tajin culture. Here the surfaces which the stone offers the tool are not treated as supporting and linking components of the sculpture, but generally as nothing more than media for genuine stone carving—a tendency which is already noticeable in the monumental steles, created in the shadow of Olmec art, found in the area later constituting the borderland between Maya and Tajin culture. Relief carvings of grand and austere simplicity, such as flank the stairway of one of the inner courtyards of the "Palacio" of Palenque, are the exception in Mayan art, where the pomp and splendour of ceremonial scenes together with the appropriate glyph-series are given such prominence that for this reason perhaps stone and stucco reliefs were produced in lavish quantities, yet hardly any sculpture in the round. Sculpture of this kind attained its highest degree of artistic achievement during the seventh and eighth centuries by our reckoning in Palenque, Yaxchilán, Piedras Negras (Guatemala) and numerous smaller cities of the Usumacinta region. The style cultivated there, graceful and lively as it often is, possesses a marked air of nobility (plates 46, 49, 50), and, with all its wealth of detail, a sense of balance and proportion in contrast with which the flowery baroque of the late period, as exemplified by the virtuoso sculptures of Quiriguá (Guatemala) and Copán (Honduras), presents a painful falling-off.

Among the sculptures of the Tajin culture certain oddly-shaped stone objects take first rank: the "Yugos", shaped like horse-shoes; the "Palmas", recalling a fan-shaped palm-frond (plates 58, 60); and the wedge-shaped "Hachas" (plates 59, 61). Opinions vary as to the sig-nificance of these carved objects, which are peculiar to the Tajin culture—the "Hachas" alone are distributed also over the isthmus side of the Pacific coast. The suggestion has lately been put forward that they may be carved replicas of emblems of the sacred ball-game used as burial offerings. Frequently the ornamentation of these objects is extremely elaborate: principally they take the form of fantastic representations of men and animals, heads and sacred motifs, pointing in particular to the sacrificial ritual, whose forms echo the intertwined ornamentation of the mature Tajin style with its volutes and decorative S-shaped loops, which in this respect too can be compared with early Chinese art. Similar ornaments, resembling luxuriating water-plants, are found on the reliefs and shrine-fragments discovered among the ruins of the Tajin.

With the advent of the Toltec era a massive style of sculpture comes into being, which has certain affinities with the art of Teotihuacán, and which, as an outcome of the dissemination of Toltec culture, spreads from the Mexican upland to Yucatán. Compact forms, with bold outlines and governed by the stone's bulk, dominate full sculptures and reliefs; not for nothing is stone carving suited to architecture (plate 76). The reliefs used for the facing of pyramid and temple walls show monotonous series of stern heraldic jaguars and eagles, and also skulls; in sculptures carved in the round preference is given to reclining mythological figures, called Chac Mool, and cubiform stylized tigers. Everywhere the sculptures are shaped with a view to fitting them into the framework of large-scale, powerful architecture. This may possibly account for a certain tendency towards the abstract which is peculiar to them (plate 77). The pilasters, the door-supports and the other sculpted elements which are part and parcel of the architectural structure bear the same characteristic impress.

The large statues found in the Huaxtec zone, the finest example of which is the youthful figure in the National Museum of Mexico (plate 66), also probably date from the late period. They are already conceived entirely as independent sculptures, even though they are never quite able to overcome a certain primitive flatness. The delicately wrought tattooing or "textile"-patterning recalls the shell carvings that have been fashioned in Huaxteca since very ancient times. As in the case of practically the whole early cultural development of this important border region of old Mexico, we are still unable to attach to its stone carvings any reliable archaeological dates. It is apparently related to Aztec sculpture, and it probably also influenced that school of sculptors to whom was due the grand and powerful finale achieved by the ancient art of Mexico.

Aztec sculpture seems to have reached maturity during the last fifty years before the fall of Tenochtitlán. Despite the systematic destruction of indigenous sculptural works by the Spanish conquerors, a large number of Aztec sculptures have since come to light, among them many works of high quality (plates 93–103). As with the Olmecs, a natural gift for sculpting seems to have been inborn in their Aztec successors. Aztec stone carvers are fond of sculptures in the round and of bulky forms. Their mature style is powerfully robust without being in any way coarse; on the contrary, it betrays a strongly developed sensitivity both in fashioning the stone —mostly porous basalt—and in graduating the various plastic values, so that even those sculptures that are cumbered with symbols lose none of their powerful simplicity. Witness, for example, the giant statue of Coatlicue (plate 93); here the dissonances of the realistically carved details which the eye simply cannot take in all at one time are united in a mighty, supernatural harmony of forms. With an equal degree of unerring skill the Aztec sculptors carve both the tremendous fictions of a religion based on fear, and such prosaic things as apes, grasshoppers, a pumpkin or cactus plants. Whatever inner meaning such carvings may have possessed, they breathe something new: delight in all the potentialities of plastic form and the ability to exploit these to the full. New also is the easy realism of the statues, which are so clearly modelled upon the common man, stoical, naïf and unaffected (plates 95–98). Here that note of popular tradition is sounded which in our opinion reflects the artistic expression of the ancient people's cult, but which is now transferred from ceramics to monumental stone carving. Free from the gloomy constraint which in other ways typifies the culture of Tenochtitlán's rulers, Aztec stone carving is invested with a vitality not hitherto achieved in the ancient art of Mexico.

The prepossession, still widely prevalent, which considers the ceramic work of early peoples to be a lesser form of artistic creation, is readily disproved in our case. Ceremonial vessels

25

and figurines, which early advanced cultures of the Ancient World preferred to fashion out of more costly materials such as metal, were in old Mexico nearly always modelled "only" in clay, and are consequently found in great numbers and often repeated. By artistic standards they are of a remarkably high quality, and in this connection—particularly in the case of ceramic figures to which we confine ourselves here—we frequently encounter local schools whose clay sculptures are singularly original and elegantly shaped, sensitive and highly expressive. That applies already to the earliest periods. The clay statuettes of the archaic-ceramic cultures, which are found everywhere in the earliest levels to yield abundant archaeological material—whose age, in the case of the Valley of Mexico, is now estimated at some three thousand years—show a number of local variations of basically common stylistic traits; amongst these may be mentioned the original and realistic rendering of the facial features, hair-dressing and ritual adornments. At the same time these various ways of presenting the basic types reveal their chronological sequence. The finds of recent years in Tlatilco go to show that certain early archaic terra-cottas— which George C. Vaillant, the outstanding explorer of the early civilizations of Mexico, has not long since described as the works of a veritable "Michelangelo" of his day—are not unique items completely departing from the norm, but derive from a specific local school whose original vivacious and imaginative style, partly as a result of unmistakable Olmec influence, acquires a particular artistic accent (plates 1–11). The clay sculptures of purely Olmec type that have been found in addition are already monumental, like the stone carvings of the mature La Venta culture; every plastic effect that can be obtained from the pliant material is thought-fully and precisely brought out in these works of art, which are also remarkable technically (plates 15, 16). The figurines of the later archaic-ceramic epoch no longer reach this high level. Even in the amusing and, in their own way original, little clay figures of Chupicuaro— a site famous for its magnificently-shaped pottery, surprising in its variety—we miss the artistic touch which enchants us again and again in the terra-cottas of Tlatilco. At what was pre-sumably a later period the archaic tradition reappears with exuberant power in the art of Colima, Nayarit and Jalisco (plates 67–75). Exuberant also in that all the standards set by the original archaic-ceramics, both in the matter of formal aspect and expression, go by the board; in that the severe and mostly symmetrical frontality is superseded by a three-dimensional aspect often still further animated by an accentuated asymmetry; and in that the delicate restraint of line is broadened into a sturdy, sometimes even uncouth one. In form, as well as in their interpretation of the object, these quite extraordinary and plastically powerful terra-cottas are bursting with vitality. The particularly varied and technically accomplished ceramics of Colima include numerous realistic representations of animals shaped into vessels, which are among the most attractive works of ancient Mexican art (plate 73).

The classic period sees the introduction of moulds, which we have already mentioned in another connection, but which of course also have their artistic consequences. The resulting changes in form and plastic content are best seen in the ceramics of the upland cultures, which in every case bear a clearly defined imprint, hardly modified by local variations. The early Teotihuacán terra-cottas, which are still modelled by hand throughout, show a surprisingly graceful interpretation which, compared with stone sculpture, is both intimate and charming (plate 30). By contrast, there is the ceramic work of Monte Albán, which in its first, still pre-classic phase betrays strongly Olmec affinities (plate 34), and only subsequently the Zapotec stylistic traits most strikingly presented in the large figural grave-urns; even that of the early period tends towards grandeur, where expression, as well as composition and size are con-cerned (plates 37, 40–42). The use of moulds originally resulted everywhere in more generous proportioning and a more elaborate fashioning of details; later, however, it led to a toning down of plastic accentuation and a loss of expressiveness. During the late period of both cultures mechanical routine ultimately gained the upper hand. The wealth of external orna-mentation only serves to emphasize the vapidness of terra-cottas resulting from series produc-tion; this applies as much to the pompously elaborate clay urns of the late Zapotec style as to the clay sculpture of Teotihuacán, where a flat, decorative pattern comes to predominate more and more.

Where the ceremonial ceramics of Teotihuacán are concerned, the smooth-faced vessels covered with paintings in a fresco-like manner and incised plano-reliefs soon occupy a special place, much as they did to a large extent in the Maya "Old Empire". Among the terra-cottas which show old Mayan art at its best, special mention must be made of the grave-figurines found on the island of Jaina (plates 52, II). Usually conceived in the round and modelled with the help of moulds, their delicacy of expression coupled with a dignified elegance clearly betray affinities with the sculptural style in vogue in Palenque. Little of comparable quality has so far come to light, though the Mayan zone which is still largely covered by jungle no doubt conceals an unbounded wealth of ceramics of all kinds. Relatively little exploration and research has also as yet been devoted to the exceptionally rich clay pottery of the Totomac zone, whose robustly realistic style was frequently carried to considerable heights of artistic achieve-ment by numerous local "schools" ascertained from Huaxteca to the frontiers of the Maya territory, and which had apparently been influenced sometimes by the art of Teotihuacán, at other times by that of Monte Albán or of the Maya. The strangely attractive, rapturous "cara sonrientes" terra-cottas (plates 63, 64) show in what an original way such influences were adapted.

Towards the end of the classic period the artistic quality of clay figurines progressively declines, becoming relatively insignificant in the post-classic period. Early in that period the pottery known as "plombate" on account of the vitreous slip obtained through the use of lead-bearing earth and which was imported from the South, found a wide distribution. The Puebla-Mixtec culture, so important for its place in the late art development of Central

Mexico, once more evinces true originality in its pottery, which reflects what might be termed the arts-and-crafts style, manifest in particular in mosaic and gold work (plates 88, 89, III), as well as in the didactic graphic display of its illuminated folding books. Decorative vase-painting leads the field (plate 90). Aztec art, too, follows this trend; its figure pottery is rather poor and lacks that feeling for form manifested in the stone carvings.

An idea of what painting was like in the classic period may be gained from the murals and vase-paintings found in Teotihuacán and the Maya region. The sure pictorial interpretation which characterizes the style common to both these cultures, the finished draughtsmanship and fine coloration, offer tangible evidence that painting was there practised as an independent branch of art. Teotihuacán painting, characterized by its decoratively broadened, symbolically stylized and ceremonially rigid style (plate 32), has its counterpart, where the art of the Maya "Old Empire" is concerned, in the epic mobility of the delicate and elegantly sketched vase-paintings of Chama (plates 53, 54) and Uaxactún (Guatemala) and the magnificent murals of Bonampák, bursting with vitality and colour. By comparison, the stereotyped wall-painting of post-classical art has nothing approaching this to offer.

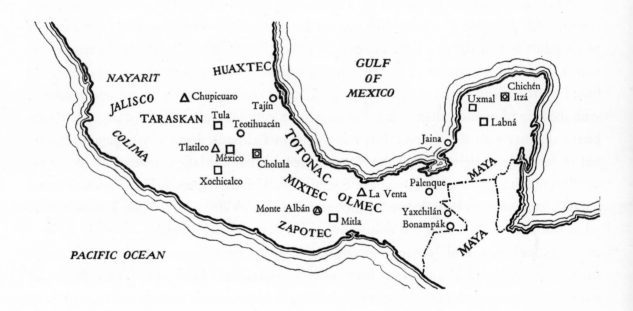

The chart overleaf indicates, in simplified form, only the principal cultures which contributed decisively to the development of ancient Mexican art. The customary subdivision of individual cultures according to phases of development—as, for example, phases I to IV of Teotihuacán or Monte Albán—which we encounter in specialist works on archaeology, has been omitted, in order to avoid obscuring the overall picture. Among the archaic-ceramic cultures, traces of which have been found in all the indicated areas of civilization, only the two principal "art centres" are shown: Tlatilco and Chupicuaro. The art of the western regions—Colima, Jalisco, Nayarit—which is associated with archaic-ceramic traditions, does not strictly fit into the framework of the chart, since its dates are still uncertain and it stands apart from the classic cultures; this entry has therefore been made in italics.

As regards the dating of the individual cultures, this follows the mostly accepted present-day views. It must be borne in mind that the first truly authenticated dates are those of the Spanish conquest; all earlier ones are relative. This applies even to the late period, whose history has in some directions been so clarified through available data, that certain historical events, such as the founding of Tenochtitlán (1325) and the destruction of Tula (1168), can be more or less exactly dated.

As pertains to the classic cultures, a chronological order, previously referred to and based upon original sources, exists for one of these—the Maya culture; in this connection the co-ordination of the Mayan calendar with our method of reckoning is relative. The years and other dates given in this book accord with the now mostly accepted correlation of Goodman-Martinez-Thompson. The broad chronological plan of the remaining classic cultures can be derived from archaeological data, from common characteristics visible in particular in architecture and art, from directly ascertainable reciprocal relationships and other analogies. The picture becomes far more complicated when approaching the beginnings and early phases of the classic cultures. The earliest Mayan date recorded in the classic manner (on the Leyden plaque) corresponds to the year A.D. 317; still older dates (going as far back as 21 B.C.) appear on various monuments and objects found in the southern Gulf zone, which, however, are in no way related stylistically to the Maya culture, and only indirectly on the strength of their inscriptions. On the other hand, archaeological finds suggest that the beginnings at least of the great ritual centres of Teotihuacán and Monte Albán date back to still earlier times.

Whereas it was possible to classify these beginnings, as well as the pre-classic cultures, the Olmec and the archaic-ceramic, according to their archaeological sequence and, consequently, to determine which preceded which—the excavations that contributed most towards gauging the general sequence of cultures were in the Valley of Mexico, and were in due course confirmed by progressive discoveries in other cultural zones—their actual dates remained a matter of guesswork. Only in recent years has the system devised by Dr. W. F. Libby of the University of Chicago, by means of which the age of certain archaeological remains is deduced from the radio-activity of the carbon isotope 14 (C 14), provided us with a scientific means of ascertaining chronological data. Investigations based upon this method have since shown that the early period of Teotihuacán and Monte Albán dates back some 2300 years, while Tlatilco appears as the oldest known archaic-ceramic culture, dating back to about 1500 B.C. That is appreciably earlier than one has hitherto ventured to place it.

29

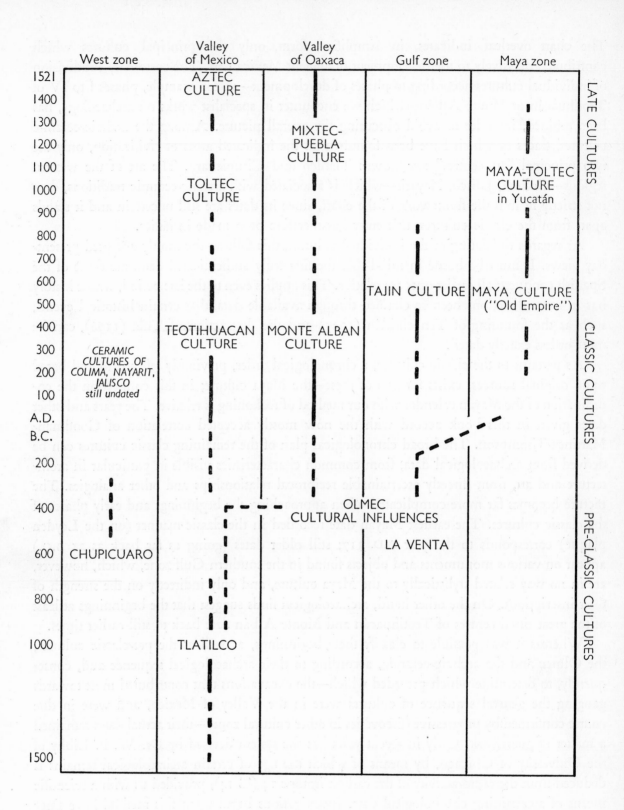

	West zone	Valley of Mexico	Valley of Oaxaca	Gulf zone	Maya zone	
1521		AZTEC CULTURE				LATE CULTURES
1400						
1300			MIXTEC-PUEBLA CULTURE			
1200						
1100		TOLTEC CULTURE			MAYA-TOLTEC CULTURE in Yucatán	
1000						
900						
800						
700						
600				TAJIN CULTURE	MAYA CULTURE ("Old Empire")	CLASSIC CULTURES
500						
400	CERAMIC CULTURES OF COLIMA, NAYARIT, JALISCO still undated	TEOTIHUACAN CULTURE	MONTE ALBAN CULTURE			
300						
200						
100						
A.D.						
B.C.						
200						
400			OLMEC CULTURAL INFLUENCES			PRE-CLASSIC CULTURES
600	CHUPICUARO			LA VENTA		
800						
1000		TLATILCO				
1500						

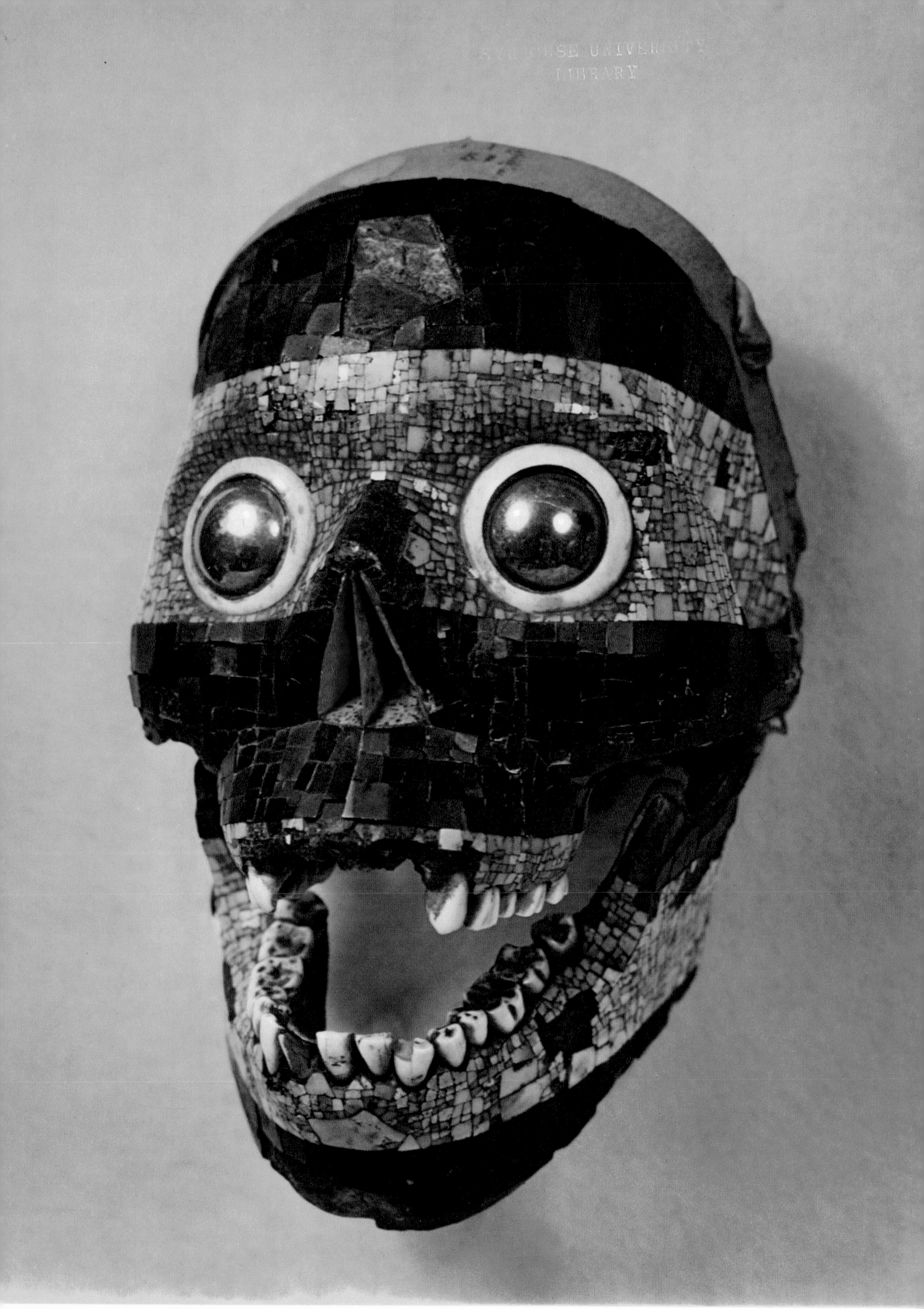

2

3

4

5

6

7

9

13

14

15

16

17

18

22

23

24

25

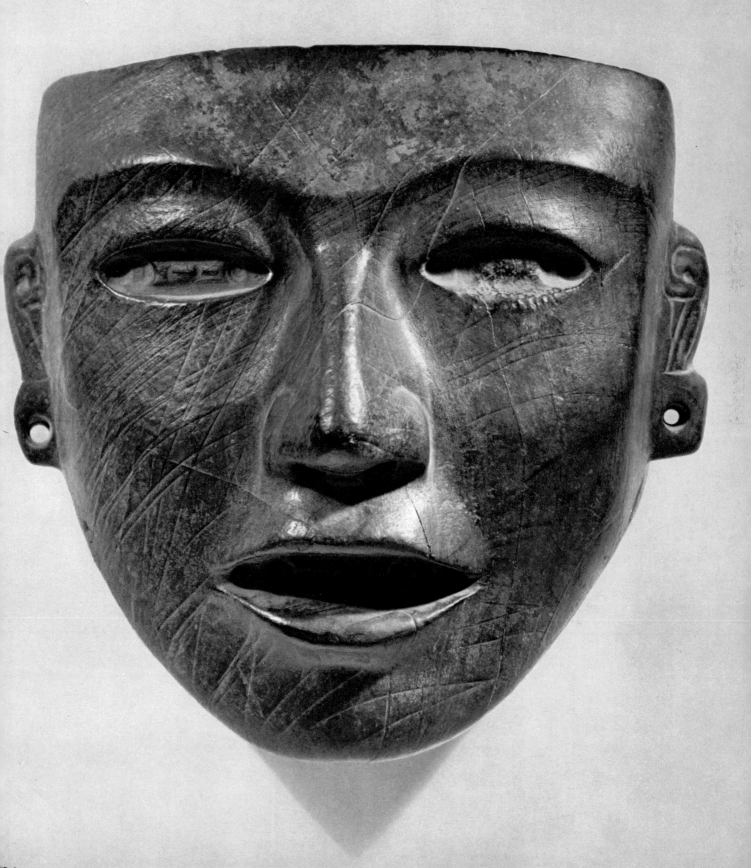

27

34

38

39

40

41

43

47

48

51

53

54

56

58

59

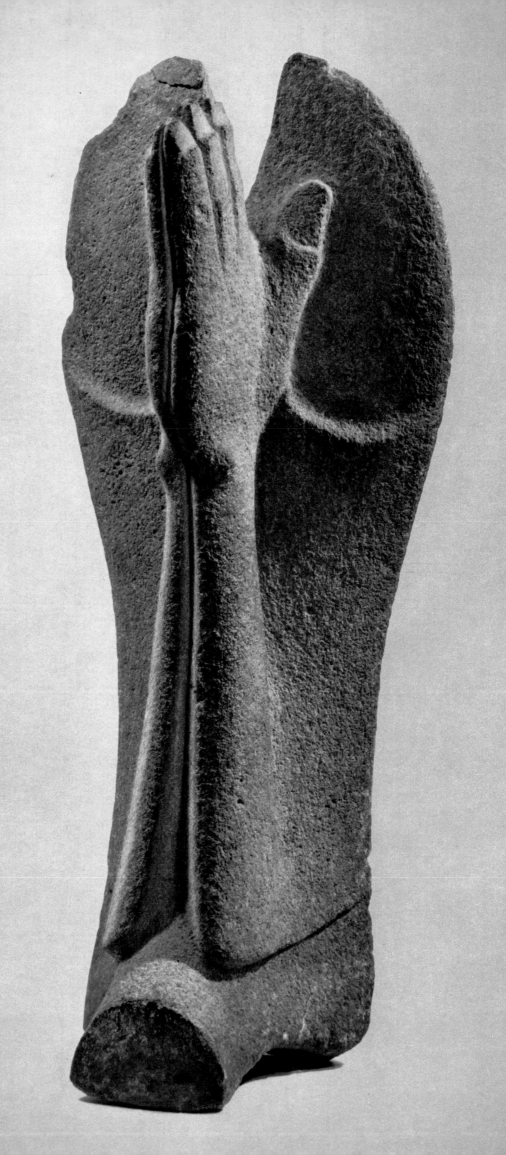

61

65

67

69

70

71

72

3

74

75

77

78

81

82

89

88

90

93

95

96

99

100

101

102

103

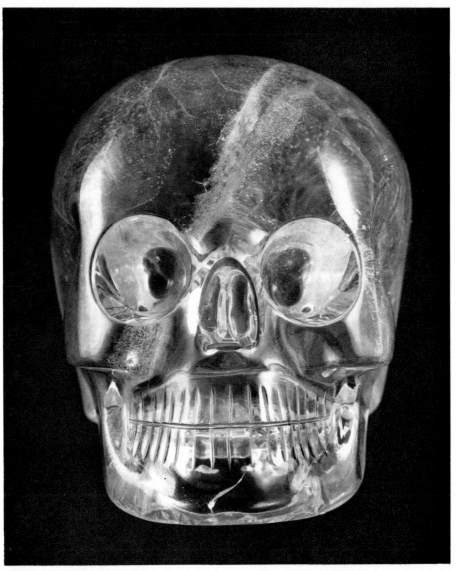

104

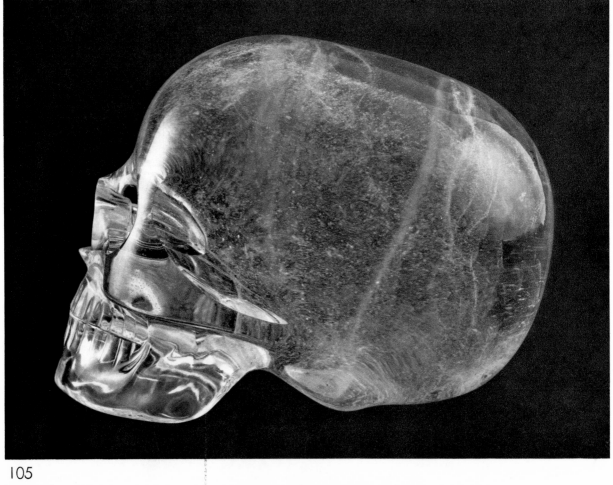

105

NOTES ON THE PLATES

Colour Plates

I OLMEC CEREMONIAL AXE. Jade. Height, 20 cm. (7⅞ in.). British Museum, London.
Stone carvings in the shape of an axe, consisting of a powerfully sculpted mask in which human and feline features intermingle, and a severely stylized body, are characteristic of Olmec art. This example shows the classical style of these carvings. (*Frontispiece.*)

II CLAY STATUE OF A MAYAN DIGNITARY, with tattooed mouth, wearing a quilted cotton wrap. Height, 27·2 cm. (10⅝ in.). Jaina. Museo Nacional, México, D.F.
Mayan priests, who appear so remote on stone and stucco reliefs when depicted in the intricacies of cere⁄monial emblems or ideographs, become more tangible and human in these small burial potteries from Jaina. (*Facing page* 10.)

III DOUBLE⁄HEADED SERPENT. Turquoise mosaic on wood; teeth and jaws encrusted with shell. Length, 44·5 cm. (17½ in.). Aztec or Mixtec. British Museum, London. (*Facing page* 18.)

IV HUMAN SKULL, encrusted with mosaic of turquoise and obsidian; eyes of iron pyrites. Height, 20 cm. (7⅞ in.). Aztec. British Museum, London.
Stone mosaic work is a prominent craft in ancient Mexico, with a tradition that goes back to early times. But nearly all the well⁄known, well⁄preserved examples are of the Mixtec or Aztec period, and some already found their way to Europe some centuries ago, as booty from the Spanish Conquest. This encrusted skull probably represents Tezcatlipoca, one of the most important and most sinister deities in Aztec mythology. (*Facing page* 30.)

Photogravure Plates

1 CLAY FIGURE OF A FEMALE DANCER, with traces of red colour. Height, 11 cm. (4⅜ in.). Tlatilco. Private Collection, Mexico, D.F.

2 PAIR OF FIGURES. Height, 9 and 9·5 cm. (3½ and 3¾ in.). Tlatilco. Private Collection, Mexico, D.F.

3 SMALL CLAY FIGURE OF A BEARDED MAN, with traces of yellow, red and white colour. Height, 10 cm. (3⅞ in.). Tlatilco. Private Collection, Mexico, D.F.

4 FEMALE FIGURE WITH TWO FACES, painted yellow. Height, 5·5 cm. (2⅛ in.). Tlatilco. Private Collection, Mexico, D.F.

5 FEMALE FIGURE WITH TWO HEADS. Black tattoo on a yellow ground. Height, 10·5 cm. (4⅛ in.). Tlatilco. Private Collection, Mexico, D.F.

6 CLAY FIGURE OF A YOUNG MAN. Height, 17·5 cm. (6⅞ in.). Tlatilco. Private Collection, Mexico, D.F.

7 FIGURE OF A DANCER, with trouser⁄like covering for the legs, and head⁄dress fastened at the back of the neck. Traces of red, yellow and white colour. Height, 15·5 cm. (6⅛ in.). Tlatilco. Private Collection, Mexico, D.F.

These terra⁄cottas from Tlatilco, originally brightly painted and tattooed, show the art of the early archaic⁄ceramic period at its liveliest and best. Although usually calling for a strictly head⁄on view, they never⁄theless show a graceful lack of restraint in form and expression; the symmetrical outline encloses movement in an original manner. Differences in physiognomy, decoration and tattooing point to the fact that these terra⁄cottas, always hand⁄modelled in the same manner, come from different tribal groups. They might have been buried as companions of the dead, showing their particular ritual dress. The double faces and heads probably reflect dualistic ideas.

8 MASK OF LIGHT POLISHED CLAY. Height, 8 cm. (3⅛ in.). Tlatilco. Private Collection, Mexico, D.F.
Among archaic burial objects there are clay masks of various sizes which might be imitations—specially modelled for the purpose—of masks used at ritual dances and made of wood or other materials. The present example combines two elements usually repre⁄sented in separate masks: the skull and a face with grotesquely opened mouth, bared teeth and drooping tongue. The pierced upper teeth in the left half of the mask point to the custom of deforming teeth artificially.

9 BLACK GLAZED CLAY VESSEL, representing a kneeling man wearing a helmet and a mask dyed red. Height, 26 cm. (10¼ in.). Tlatilco. Private Collection, Mexico, D.F.

The larger burial terra-cottas of the archaic period are hollow figures or vessels in the shape of animals or men. The helmet of the figure here represented is in the shape of a duck's head with its beak turned towards the nape of the neck. The mask shows the face of a withered old man, of which occasional examples appear already at this period, and which later becomes generally associated with the god of fire. Body-belt and loin-cloth are indicated by incised lines.

10 BLACK GLAZED CLAY BOWL, in the shape of a fish. Fins and belly originally coloured red. Height, 13·3 cm. (5¼ in.). Tlatilco, Museo Nacional, México, D.F.

11 VASE IN THE SHAPE OF A DUCK. Brown-black glaze. Height, 17 cm. (6¾ in.). Tlatilco. Private Collection, Mexico, D.F.

The sensitively rendered vessels in the shape of animals, depicting fishes, toads, rodents, wild boars and ducks, are probably connected with ancient totemic conceptions. The duck in particular seems to have been a highly revered object, as is also shown by representations of human beings masked and disguised with duck emblems.

12 COLOSSAL HEAD IN BASALT. Monument No. 1 at La Venta, Tabasco. Total height, c. 270 cm. (106¼ in.). Among the great monolithic stone sculptures of the various ritual sites which the American archaeologist M. W. Stirling excavated between 1939 and 1941 south of Vera Cruz, in the Mexican Gulf zone leading to the primeval swamps of Tabasco, the colossal heads bearing the genuine features of Olmec sculpture are especially notable. The name of the most important site, La Venta, where, apart from several of these monuments, huge altars, steles and other relics in the same style have been found, has since been applied by experts to the culture previously designated as Olmec. So far, as little light has been shed on the significance of these gigantic heads, always adorned with a helmet-like head-dress, as on nearly everything else connected with the historical, ethnic or cultural backgrounds of the Olmec or La Venta civilization,

a civilization which is now considered to be the cradle of the great ceremonial sculpture of ancient Mexico.

13 SQUATTING MALE FIGURE, with arms bent in front of his chest (ball-player?). Basalt. Height, 65 cm. (25⅝ in.). La Venta district. Private Collection, Mexico, D.F.

14 BACK VIEW OF THE SAME FIGURE.

Among the many excellent Olmec sculptures so far discovered, this is artistically the most significant and impressive. Whether the figure—one of the most important items in the Exhibition of Mexican Art shown in Paris, Stockholm and London in 1952–53—should be called "The Wrestler", the name given to it in the catalogue, seems doubtful, however. More probably, it represents a participant in the sacred ball-game, which has been traced back to a very early period in ancient Mexico. In this the players, protected by a special belt, had to parry a massive rubber ball with their hips.

15 WHITE GLAZED CLAY FIGURE, with child-like features. Height, 36·6 cm. (14⅜ in.). Tlatilco. Private Collection, Mexico, D.F.

16 SEATED FIGURE. Clay, with traces of white glaze. Height, 18 cm. (7⅛ in.). Tlatilco. Private Collection, Mexico, D.F.

Olmec clay figurines found in Tlatilco prove that Olmec artists were as accomplished in this medium as they were when working in stone. The discovery of such ceramics in Tlatilco confirms the antiquity of this enigmatic civilization and proves that the La Venta style was already fully developed in Central Mexico at this early period.

17 OLMEC JADE FIGURE of a weeping dwarf or child. Height, 12·1 cm. (4¾ in.). Cerro de las Mesas. Museo Nacional, México, D.F.

18 SEATED JADE FIGURE, dyed red, with a pyrite disk attached to the chest. Height, 7·5 cm. (3 in.). La Venta. Museo Nacional, México, D.F.

The Olmecs were unsurpassed masters in the carving of jade—a substance which was prized beyond all others in ancient Mexico. The fact that small Olmec jades, found as far apart as Central Mexico and Costa Rica, were scattered over a wide area, and that "treasure hoards" of definitely later date contained Olmec jade work, indicates that even in early times these objects must have been considered as especially precious and passed down from hand to hand.

19 MASK OF GREEN STONE. Height, 14·3 cm. (5⅝ in.). Mexican Gulf. Museo Nacional, México, D.F.
One of the most striking examples of the realistic way in which Olmec sculptors represented the human face. The eyes, as is commonly found in old Mexican stone masks, were originally inlaid with material of a different colour.

20 WHITE GLAZED CLAY HEAD, with hair coloured red. Height, 14 cm. (5½ in.). Origin unknown. Museo Nacional, México, D.F.
Probably a fragmemt of a seated figure. Within the general framework of Olmec characteristics of modelling, the facial features show a definite affinity with the archaic style of Tlatilco.

21 PLAQUE OF DARK GREEN STONE. Height, 13 cm. (5⅛ in.). Mexican Gulf. Museo Nacional, México, D.F.
The large head in profile on this plaque, which might have been made as a pectoral, shows the curved mouth with intermingling human and feline features, characteristic of many Olmec works of art. A comparison should be made between the profile set into the top of the skull and the three other engraved profiles of jaguar masks. The stylized, V-shaped incision into the skull is found in much Olmec sculpture. The dug-out parts of the plaque may originally have been inlaid with a different material.

22 VASE OF LIGHT POLISHED CLAY, with engraved head motifs, toned brown. Height, 20 cm. (7⅞ in.). Valley of Mexico. Private Collection, Mexico, D.F.
The decorations make this an interesting companion to plate 21. So far very few Olmec ceramics are known which are characterized by flat bottoms and straight sides—rendering them more suitable for pictorial decoration—as against the typical archaic round shapes imitating the husks of fruit.

23 THE PYRAMID OF THE SUN AT TEOTIHUACÁN. Front view.

About 65 m. (213 ft.) high, upon an almost square base with sides of over 200 m. (656 ft.) the sun pyramid is the most important building in the large ruined ceremonial city of Teotihuacán. Although the reconstruction of 1905–10 was not entirely satisfactory, the monument even in its present form illustrates the impressive, broadly powerful architecture of Teotihuacán, which seems to be fitted to the massive contours of the mountains that border the horizon.

24 WALL DECORATION ON THE PYRAMID OF QUETZAL-COATL AT TEOTIHUACÁN. Detail.
The fantastic heads which jut out from a background adorned with fertility and water emblems show, in symbolic combination, now the realistic features of jaguars and snakes, now the abstract forms of the mask of the rain god and the butterfly.

25 MASK OF DARK SLATE. Height, 19·3 cm. (7⅝ in.). Cholula. Private Collection, Mexico, D.F.

26 MASK OF BROWNISH STONE. Height, 21·5 cm. (8½ in.). Valley of Mexico. Private Collection, Mexico, D.F.
The block-shaped, realistic stone masks which are among the most noble and impressive of ancient Mexican works of art, are characteristic of Teotihuacán sculpture. Eyes and mouth were originally inlaid with differently coloured material and the ears were pierced so that small discs of jade could be fastened to them. It is conjectured that such masks were applied to the shrouds of nobles at the ceremonial display.

27 SEATED ALABASTER FIGURE. Height, 26 cm. (10¼ in.). Teotihuacán. Private Collection, Mexico, D.F.
The severe harmony of forms focuses the attention on the face, the most important part of the sculpture. The Teotihuacán style emphasized horizontal lines even in its smaller sculptures.

28 PAIR OF TERRA-COTTA FIGURES, depicting dwarfs decorated with feathers. Traces of yellow, white and dark red colour. Height, 17 and 18 cm. (6¾ and 7⅛ in.). Teotihuacán. Museo Nacional, México, D.F.

29 MOTHER WITH CHILD. Clay, painted white, yellow and red. Height, 8 cm. (3⅛ in.). Ahuizotla. Private Collection, Mexico, D.F.

30 CLAY FIGURE OF A CHILD, with ribbon-like head decoration. Traces of yellow, red and white colour. Height, 12 cm. (4¾ in.). Ahuizotla. Private Collection, Mexico, D.F.

These small clay sculptures illustrate the change from the early, hand-modelled Teotihuacán terra-cottas (plate 30) to the later figures made from moulds (plate 28). The figure shown on plate 29 is of the transition period: the head and upper part of the woman's body have been made with the aid of a mould, the remaining parts are modelled by hand.

31 SACRIFICIAL ONYX BOWL, in the shape of an ocelot. Length, 33 cm. (13 in.). Teotihuacán. British Museum, London.

A comparison with the fresco below will show the Teotihuacán artist's ability to depict the same object in both pictorial and sculptural terms. But the detail—as in the hairy spikes on the legs—shows that the stylization is basically the same.

32 JAGUAR WITH FEATHER DECORATION. Fresco at Teotihuacán.

Detail from a mural painting in various shades of red, depicting scenes from the ritual of the water god. A spiral scroll, signifying speech or song, rises from the mouth of the jaguar; below is an emblem symbolizing water. Teotihuacán sacred art is often rigidly dogmatic and didactically intent on representing a multitude of symbolic detail. This may be another reason why it prefers the medium of the fresco to that of stone relief, practised by other cultures. The basic colours, too, have a sacred and symbolic meaning.

33 SANDSTONE RELIEF OF A "DANZANTE". Monte Albán.

During the excavation of one of the oldest temple structures of Monte Albán, a number of stone slabs were found on which figures making grotesque movements were cut in relief. These, called "Los Danzantes"—the dancers—are among the oldest examples of Central American monumental sculpture, and their style clearly manifests Olmec influence. Especially interesting from an archaeological point of view are the ancient glyphs which are connected with the figures—in this case appearing on the left above the raised arm—and which have not so far been deciphered.

34 GREY POLISHED URN in the shape of a head. Height 15·7 cm. (6⅛ in.). Monte Negro. Museo Nacional México, D.F.

35 VASE OF BLACK POLISHED CLAY, representing a jaguar. Height, 21·5 cm. (8⅛ in.). Coxtocan. Museo Nacional, México, D.F.

The ceramic art of the earliest Monte Albán culture still bears an unmistakably archaic character, showing strong Olmec influence as well as many points of resemblance with the Tlatilco style. There is an abundance of ceremonial pottery, consisting of ingeniously decorated vessels and plates, but figures are rare. The form of the urn, predominant in later Monte Albán ceremonial ceramic art, is already used.

36 VIEW OF A SECTION OF THE CENTRAL SQUARE OF MONTE ALBÁN.

The religious centre of Monte Albán, which is today one of the most important archaeological sites on the American continent, is situated on an artificially levelled mountain plateau overlooking the Valley of Oaxaca. According to recent archaeological research, this imposing architectural centre dates back to the first millenium B.C. and points to centuries of building activity. The Zapotecs, the traditional inhabitants of this region, seem to have settled at Monte Albán during a period following the decline of an earlier civilization—whose art bears both archaic and pronounced Olmec features—and remained there as masters until the end of classical times. The excavations which have been conducted since 1931, under the direction of Alfonso Caso, have led to important discoveries concerning the development of ancient Central American civilizations.

37 BURIAL FIGURE REPRESENTING A DIGNITARY WITH CEREMONIAL ADORNMENT. With traces of colour. Height, 41·5 cm. (16⅜ in.). Monte Albán. Museo Nacional, México, D.F.

Zapotec stone sculpture is practically unknown, yet there are many clay sculptures, often of a large size, which, like this terra-cotta dating from the second period, strike a definite monumental note. Frequently the mouth and eyes of these clay figures were inlaid with shell and other materials in the manner usually associated with stone sculpture.

38 MASK WITH EMBLEMS OF THE BAT DEITY. Dark green jade. Eyes and teeth are inlaid with shell; the beard is of slate. Height, without beard, 24 cm. (9½ in.); height of beard, 28·3 cm. (11⅛ in.). Monte Albán. Museo Nacional, México, D.F.
The style is of the second Monte Albán period. The mask, the most important piece of jade sculpture yet found at Monte Albán, is made of several smaller pieces, carefully joined together. The formation of forehead, nose and cheeks would indicate that a human face, decorated with the mask of the bat deity, is depicted. The bat is associated with the cult of the maize deity and is constantly returning in the representational art of Monte Albán.

39 CLAY URN in the shape of a bat's head. Height, 37·5 cm. (14¾ in.). Monte Albán. Museo Nacional, México, D.F.
In this case the animal's head is depicted with all its characteristic features. The original effectiveness and fierce vitality of these ceramics was undoubtedly further heightened by the bold colouring and the inlaid eyes.

40 CLAY URN in the shape of a figure, with engraved decoration. Height, 31·7 cm. (12½ in.). Monte Albán. Private Collection, Mexico, D.F.

41 CLAY URN representing the goddess "Z 8" (so called after the glyph engraved in her lap), wearing a mask in the shape of a serpent. Height, 40 cm. (15¾ in.). Monte Albán. Museo Nacional, México, D.F.

42 CLAY URN representing a richly dressed, bearded old man. Height, 46·7 cm. (18⅜ in.). Monte Albán. Private Collection, Mexico, D.F.
These urns are in the mature style of the second and early third period. Generously and expressively modelled, they are as yet free from the stamp of routine and decorative formalism which many of the later clay sculptures bear. Funerary urns in the form of figures, with cylindrical vessels at the back, are typical of Monte Albán pottery. These did not serve as receptacles for the remains of the dead but were put up as burial offerings in the funeral vaults frequently found in Monte Albán and other Zapotec districts.

43 TEMPLE OF THE SUN AT PALENQUE.
A few years ago work was begun to win back the temple town of Palenque—renowned for its beauty among travellers and explorers since the beginning of the nineteenth century—from the jungle forests, and to explore and rebuild it. In the course of this a great number of surprising archaeological and artistic discoveries were made. In the seventh century A.D. Palenque played an important role among the metropolises of the "Old Empire" of the Maya. This is proved by the abundance of its inscriptions and the refinement of its art and architecture, which, in many respects, are considered to be unsurpassed in the culture of the Old Maya Empire. The so-called Temple of the Sun, which, with two similar temples, borders three sides of a ceremonial square, is the best preserved building of the classic Maya period. The interior consists of two naves running parallel to the front face and spanned by corbelled arches. The back nave contains the inner chamber, which has a dedicatory relief with a date corresponding to the year 692 in our era, let into the back wall. Only traces now remain of the painted stucco relief which originally adorned the façade and the ornamental roof-crest—so typical of Old Mayan architecture.

44 TEMPLE OF INSCRIPTIONS AT PALENQUE.
This takes its name from the tablets in the interior of the temple which are covered entirely with glyphs carved in relief, and which also give a date of dedication corresponding to the year 692. The roof and roof-crest have fallen in and the stucco reliefs of the exterior have been almost completely destroyed. A staircase descending into the base of the pyramid leads to the unique burial chamber discovered in 1952.

45 SCULPTED STAIRWAY ENCLOSURE FROM THE "PALACIO" AT PALENQUE.
One of the staircases of the "Palacio", descending into the monumental inner court on the north side, is enclosed by great sculpted square stones. The figures in relief, which are larger than life-size and depart from the otherwise graceful and elegant style of Palenque reliefs in their massive solidity, may date from a time preceding the period of artistic maturity. A date corresponding to the year 603 by our reckoning is cut into the steps of the facing staircase.

46 STELE CARVED IN RELIEF, from Balam-Kan. Height of group of figures c. 125 cm. (49¼ in.). Museo de Villahermosa, Tabasco.

Steles in the form of stone blocks cut into rectangular shapes and decorated with sculptures, are among the most frequent cult monuments of the "Old Empire" of the Maya. Inscriptions and pictorial representations are usually related to commemorative dates in the sacred calendar, or to ceremonial occasions. Other subjects are only rarely illustrated, as in this relief depicting the martial victory of a Mayan dignitary and distinguished by its forceful composition.

47-48 INITIALS OF A GLYPH SERIES CARVED IN THE FORM OF FULL FIGURES. Height, 24 cm. (9½ in.). Palenque. Details from the tablet of fine limestone, carved in relief, which was found in 1949 in the "Palacio" and ranks among the most beautiful monuments of its kind. These full figure initials, of which only a few examples are known, are attached to the head of glyph series, and depict so-called "period bearers". The periods are personified by animals or fantastic creatures and supported by the gods of the numbers by which these periods were distinguished. The date of dedication of this wonderful tablet in three sections corresponds to the year 672 in our reckoning.

49 DETAIL from the dedicatory relief tablet in the Temple of the Foliated Cross at Palenque. Limestone. Height of figure, 180 cm. (70⅞ in.).
The tablet from which this detail is taken shows a plant—probably maize—opening up in the form of a cross, decorated with symbolical masks and heads, and flanked by two worshippers and rows of glyphs. Again the date of dedication corresponds to the year 692. Like all sculpture of this kind, this relief with its extraordinarily delicate yet precise carving was originally coloured.

50 HEAD OF A YOUTH, with lavish head decoration. Stucco, with traces of red colour. Height, 39 cm. (15⅜ in.).
From the burial chamber of the Temple of Inscriptions at Palenque, excavated in 1952. This stucco sculpture, which probably dates from the first third of the seventh century, shows the mature style of Palenque—especially distinguished by its finely characterized portrait heads and masks—at its best. In the sarcophagus of the burial chamber an artificial nose adornment of jade was found among many other funeral implements in this precious material, which may explain the extended

bridge of the nose so strikingly depicted in the portraits of the classic Maya.

51 CLAY URN WITH SEATED FIGURE. Teapa. Height, 60·5 cm. (23⅞ in.). Museo de Villahermosa, Tabasco. Clay sculptures of this kind were placed in the caves as sacred offerings. A point of interest is the background to the figure posing between fantastic masks, made up of Baroquely twisting foliage in which small romping figures (the heads have been broken off) are entwined. Such stylistic forms in the art of the Old Maya Empire recently caused a discussion of the possibility of a link with the cultural sphere of southeast Asia.

52 CLAY FIGURE with traces of colour. Jaina. Height, 18 cm. (7⅛ in.). Museo de Villahermosa, Tabasco. Many of the finest terra-cottas of the classic period in Mayan art were found on the island of Jaina, near Campeche. Elegance of form, precise and delicate direction of line, and expressive characterization of the heads, put these small, exquisitely modelled tomb sculptures on a level with the masterpieces of Mayan stone and stucco sculpture.

53-54 PAINTED CLAY BEAKER. Nebaj (Guatemala). Height, c. 15 cm. (5⅞ in.). British Museum, London. The faded paintwork—red and black on a pale yellow background—depicts a dignitary, seated on a kind of raised litter, receiving offerings from two persons (a similar ceremonial scene with two figures is illustrated on the other side, not shown here). Each figure is preceded by a series of glyphs. Only a few painted vessels have been sufficiently well preserved to give an idea of the quality of vase-painting in the "Old Empire". The colours are chiefly intended to heighten the contrast and the illusion of reality created by the extraordinarily fluent draughtsmanship.

55 SEATED CLAY FIGURE of a dignitary in ornamental dress. Simojovel. Height, 29 cm. (11⅜ in.). Private Collection, Mexico, D.F.
This impressive terra-cotta demonstrates the air of authority with which the Mayan hierarchy could surround itself, especially when represented in the act of devotion. The pompous ceremonial dress further stresses this note.

56 CLAY BOWL in the form of a shell, with panel of symbolical ornaments. Exterior, dull white glaze, interior, orange glaze. Frontera. Height, 15 cm. (5⅞ in.). Museo de Villahermosa, Tabasco.
The noble form represents a stylized shell, emblem of the earth's interior, fertility and birth.

57 THE NICHE-PYRAMID OF TAJIN.
This pyramid is the most striking building that has so far been cleared in the large ruined city of Tajin (the name is popular in origin but has become the current archaeological designation for the classical culture of the Mexican Gulf). The upper platform, which carried the richly carved temple, reaches a height of 18 m. (59⅝ ft.). The unusual effect of the pyramid is due to the stone panelling which forms altogether 365 niches. The niche as a special architectural motif also appears on other Tajin buildings. The step pattern terminating in a volute, one of the most prevalent ceremonial decorative elements in ancient Mexico, especially in later times, which has been interpreted in a number of different ways, is worked into the stair enclosure. In spite of its obvious links with neighbouring cultures—architecturally with Teotihuacán and decoratively with Mayan art—the Tajin style strikes a characteristically individual note. The origins of this style have still to be traced as has the development of Tajin culture as a whole.

58 PALMA, made of andesite, representing a human sacrificial victim with gaping chest wound. Mexican Gulf. Height, 58 cm. (22⅞ in.). Museo Nacional, México, D.F.
These stone sculptures, which spread out fanwise towards the top and are found only in the orbit of the Tajin civilization, are called "Palma". Their significance is not known. The carving, whether representing figures or purely abstract decoration, is usually richly ornate, corresponding to the luxuriant and dynamic design of the "Tajin" style.

59 HACHA, made of andesite, depicting an acrobat. Mexican Gulf. Height, c. 35 cm. (13¾ in.). Private Collection, Mexico, D.F.
These flat, axe-shaped stone sculptures, too, are particularly characteristic of Tajin culture. The nude figure of an acrobat which is represented on this "Hacha" appears in very similar form in terra-cottas

from Tlatilco, as well as on a stone relief from Palenque. Presumably these jugglers also performed for ceremonial purposes.

60 PALMA, made of basalt, in the form of two folded hands and forearms. Mexican Gulf. Height, 41·5 cm. (16⅜ in.). Private Collection, Mexico, D.F.
The pose of this sculpture, which is conceived with unusual nobility and simplicity, may arouse feelings in the spectator today which are very far removed from the original meaning. Most probably the outstretched arms were those of a victim dedicated for sacrifice.

61 HACHA, made of diorite, representing a human head wearing a helmet in the shape of a marine animal. Mexican Gulf. Height, 28 cm. (11 in.). Private Collection, Mexico, D.F.
The same stylized fish, covering the top of the head like a helmet, is to be found in Mayan art. This combination of human heads and animals is frequently found on "Hachas". The cut-out decorative ribbons and eyes were presumably inlaid with material of a different colour.

62 HEAD FRAGMENT OF A CLAY FIGURE, with traces of colour. Mexican Gulf. Private Collection, Mexico, D.F.
The style of these elaborate Totonac figure ceramics is less restricted by formal canons. One of its special characteristics is the directness of form and expression which in many cases has a coarsening effect but in others lends these clay figures—originally covered with natural bitumen—a strong artistic note.

63 "CARA SONRIENTE"—CLAY FIGURE. Mexican Gulf. Height, 42 cm. (16½ in.). Private Collection, Mexico, D.F.

64 "CARA SONRIENTE"—HEAD FRAGMENT. Mexican Gulf. Height, 15 cm. (5⅞ in.). Private Collection, Mexico, D.F.
These head fragments, usually called "caras sonrientes" or "smiling faces", have been known and admired for a long time. It was only recently, however, that several complete hollow figures of this type were found. They seem to depict dancers, or perhaps victims chosen for sacrificial death. The mysterious smile which seems to hover round the heads becomes an expression of

ecstasy when the whole figure—with the head thrown back as in a state of rapture—is viewed. These peculiar, admirably modelled terra-cottas are found in the Totonac zone in slightly varied versions, and show certain affinities with Mayan ceramic art.

65 PAINTED CLAY BOWL, supported by three bulbous feet. Mexican Gulf. Diameter, c. 25 cm. (9⅞ in.). Private Collection.
The central figure is an insect-like creature, dancing before what appears to be a blossom. The painting is in black, rust, orange and white on a cream-coloured ground. Mexican Gulf pottery south of Vera Cruz often shows an interesting mixture of Totonac and Mayan features. The design, too, is reminiscent of the draughtsmanship of Mayan ceramic decoration in the crispness of its drawing.

66 THE ADOLESCENT; sandstone figure. Tamuin. Height, 141 cm. (55½ in.). Museo Nacional, México, D.F.
The figure, parts of which are covered with a finely carved tattoo, carries on its back a child with drooping head, interpreted as a symbol of the "young sun". The large stone figures from the Huaxtec region, among which this statue takes front rank, belong to the most important round sculptures of ancient Mexico. The dating of these sculptures, too, must be left to future research into the civilization of the ancient peoples of the Huaxtec region.

67 SEATED CLAY FIGURE. Reddish brown glaze, with leaf-shaped neck decoration. Colima. Height, 50 cm. (19⅝ in.). Private Collection, Mexico, D.F.
The ancient art of the western districts of Central Mexico continues the traditional archaic-ceramic style of clay sculpture which, in other parts of ancient Mexico, was being replaced by new ceremonial styles. The hollow figures frequently found in the subterranean burial chambers are completely unorthodox when considered by the standards usually applied to ancient Mexican art; sculpturally they achieve their main effect by powerful outlines and an originality and freedom of handling which sometimes strike one as almost expressionistic.

68 CLAY FIGURE with helmet and bat. Jalisco. Height, 31 cm. (12¼ in.). Private Collection, Mexico, D.F.
The figure represents a warrior or participant in a ball-game, wearing some protective body-covering which cannot be more closely identified. It shows with what natural ease movement was rendered and made into a sculptural element by the potters of ancient Western Mexico.

69 SEATED FIGURE ON A STOOL. Colima. Height, 36 cm. (14⅛ in.). Private Collection, Mexico, D.F.
The arm, with the elbow resting on the right knee, terminates in a stylized hand, which is evidently intended to support some object. The upper arms are tattooed with scars. Notwithstanding the broken left half of the body, this is one of the most interesting and impressive of the numerous and varied terra-cottas found in ancient Western Mexican culture.

70 VESSEL IN ABSTRACT FORM, supported by a snake. Colima. Height, 19·4 cm. (7⅝ in.). Private Collection, Mexico, D.F.
According to the interpretation of the Mexican art historian Salvador Toscano, this represents the trunk of a sacrificial victim. The "surrealistic" vessels from Colima, which are unique in the art of ancient Mexico, show a highly original development of archaic forms.

71 VESSEL CARRIER. Reddish glaze. 16·4 cm. long (6½ in.). Private Collection, Mexico, D.F.
In ceramics from Colima we frequently encounter figures carrying vessels on their backs or shoulders. In this case the figure, on all fours and carrying an upright amphora, appears to be a child. The band round the forehead, for pulling weights, is still used by native carriers today.

72 VESSEL IN THE SHAPE OF A DOG, with human mask. Red-brown glaze. Colima. 20·3 × 36·8 cm. (8 × 14½ in.). Museo Nacional, México, D.F.

73 VESSEL IN THE FORM OF A RESTING DOG. Colima. Height, 21 cm. (8¼ in.). Private Collection, Mexico, D.F.
Among the terra-cottas of Colima, always depicted in the form of receptacles, dogs are particularly prevalent. The realism of the plastic representation reflects an intimate observation of nature. In ancient Mexico the dog personified the deity of death and took the role of companion to those who were departing for another life. Dogs with human masks are already found in the pottery of archaic times.

74 SEATED FEMALE FIGURE. Reddish-yellow glaze. Nayarit. Height, 20 cm. (7⅞ in.). Private Collection, Mexico, D.F.
Ceramics from Nayarit are rather coarse in comparison with the style of Colima and Jalisco, but they are often characterized by an exuberant vitality. They impress by their dramatic effect, which is underlined by what to our eyes appears to be a slight leaning towards the grotesque.

75 THE CEREMONIAL BALL-GAME. Group modelled in clay. Traces of white, yellow and black colour. Nayarit. 40×25 cm. (15¾×9⅞ in.). Private Collection, Mexico, D.F.
A characteristic feature of Nayarit art is the occasional anecdotal note reflected in such terra-cotta groups, from which we can gain important information about the customs and rituals of the time. The two hut-like temples at either end of the playing-field, which is lined with spectators, should be noted. They show the original architectural form common to all sacred community buildings; the large-scale architectural edifices of classic cultures, such as as the Temple of the Sun at Palenque, were later based on it.

76 TULA. View from the decorated wall at the foot of the pyramid of Quetzalcoatl, towards the north-eastern corner of the ceremonial district of the ancient town.
In the background are the remains of the outer wall which enclosed the ball-game. The caryatids and carved posts, which presumably supported the temple erected on the upper platform of the pyramid, were found in fragments in rubble from the pyramid and were set up in front of it. The sculptures represent warriors in ornate ceremonial dress—a new theme which is appropriate to the culture of the militant Toltecs. Tula is considered the centre of the Toltec culture, which towards the end of the tenth century marks the starting-point of a new era in the history of old Mexican civilizations. The destruction of the town by barbaric tribes pushing on from the north, is now supposed to have occurred in A.D. 1168. The systematic excavation of Tula was begun in 1940.

77 STYLIZED HEAD OF A MACAW. Basalt sculpture from Xochicalco. Height, 57 cm. (22½ in.). Museo Nacional, México, D.F.
In its lapidary stylization this head strikingly embodies

the new spirit of sculpture, designed as an element within the large-scale architecture which made its appearance with Toltec art. A comparison from this point of view should be made between the sculpture here shown and the "Hacha" of plate 61, which is very similar in form.

78 SIDE WALL OF THE PYRAMID OF XOCHICALCO. Detail.
The large frieze which covers the sides of the pyramid represents plumed serpents with arched backs and seated figures fitted into the curves. Reliefs from Xochicalco appear to be influenced by the art of the Maya in both content and style. Other discoveries from the ruined sacred city, situated on the route leading from the Valley of Mexico to the Pacific coast and still in the early stages of excavation, also point to this influence.

79 TEMPLE OF KUKULKAN AT CHICHÉN ITZÁ.
Without any archaeological reason, the name of this restored temple has been associated in modern times with the name of the mythical hero of the Toltecs, known as Quetzalcoatl in Central Mexico. The pyramid, 24 m. (78¾ ft.) high, corresponds with the architectural principles of the highland cultures; the temple is covered with a flat roof without the roof-crest typical of the classic Maya period. A rather late super-structure, this pyramid temple covers—in a manner resembling the "Temple of the Warriors"—an older, smaller and very similar pyramid; one which already shows, too, the characteristics of the Maya-Toltec style.

80 THE BALL-GAME OF CHICHÉN ITZÁ. Portion of the sacred building on the edge of the square.
For two hundred years Chichén Itzá formed the centre of new political and cultural influences which made themselves felt after the end of the tenth century in the northern part of the peninsula of Yucatán, and introduced the period known as the "New Empire" of the Maya, which came to an end with the Spanish conquest in 1539. The decisive influence which, according to native tradition, the warrior tribes of the Mexican Highlands, and especially the Toltecs, exercised in Yucatán at this time, has in the meantime been confirmed by archaeology. The architecture and art of Chichén Itzá at that period correspond above all to the forms established by the Toltecs in Tula. The

massive solidity of the buildings and their sculptural ornamentation is completely "Mexican" and thus far removed from the style of the classic Maya period.

81 "TEMPLE OF THE WARRIORS" AT CHICHÉN ITZÁ. This complex of buildings, consisting of the temple itself and the porticoes which enclose its pyramid on two sides, takes its name from the pilasters (in foreground of picture) which are carved in relief with warriors in the Tula style. Buildings with flat roofs, resting on supports or pillars, are unknown in Old Maya architecture and are another manifestation of the now established "Mexican" style.

82 THE "NUNNERY" AT UXMAL. Portion of the north side of the "Casa de las Monjas", which consists of a number of buildings surrounding a large inner court. In contrast to the severe Maya-Toltec style of Chichén Itzá stands the so-called Puuc style, which appears in the architecture of other metropolises of the "New Empire". This is linked—especially in its decorative aspect—with baroque tendencies in the period of decline in classic Mayan art. A characteristic of this style is the partial or total covering of the outer walls of buildings with masonry fitted together like mosaic work, in which fantastic masks of serpents frequently form the principal decorative element. In this connection, note the two vertical panels which form part of the façade of the receding main building and originally supported a flat roof.

83 SCULPTURAL FRAGMENT from a building in Uxmal. The conventional motif of a human head enclosed by the jaws of a serpent finds particularly powerful and ornamental expression in this sculpture, called "The Queen of Uxmal". The right half of the face bears tattoo marks. Heads such as this show us the physiognomy of the ruling Mexican conquerors: a type which, compared with portraits of the classic Maya period, is harder and of a barbaric arrogance.

84 THE ARCH OF LABNA. View from the interior.

85 A PORTION OF THE PALACE OF LABNA. The ruins of Labna reveal the Puuc style at the height of its development. The lavish stone moulding of the walls is hardly excelled by the ornamentation of the temple exteriors of south-east Asia. The great arch of

one of the buildings is constructed as a false arch in the classic manner of the Mayas.

86 THE PALACE OF COLUMNS AT MITLA. The cupolas in the background belong to a church dating from the eighteenth century.

87 PORTION OF ONE OF THE INNER CHAMBERS. The old Mitla is recognized as the metropolis of the Mixtecs who took over the inheritance of the rulers of Monte Albán in the ninth century. The buildings of Mitla, which date from a later period in Mixtec civilization, show the general architectonic and decorative principles of the post-classic epoch adapted to the specific style of Mixtec art. The friezes of the stone mosaic which adorn the outer walls as well as the—by now spacious—inner chambers, are among the most beautiful examples of the geometric-decorative style which is typical of Mixtec art. The symbolic step motif is represented.

88 GOLD PECTORAL. Height, 11 cm. (4⅜ in.). Museo Regional de Oaxaca. The head represents the mask of the god of death, wearing a ceremonial head ornament; the two lower plates are each adorned with a glyph.

89 GOLD PENDANT. Museo Regional de Oaxaca. The different links, which are decorated in a kind of filigree pattern typical of the work of the Mixtec goldsmiths, represent (from top to bottom): two ballplayers, the sun disc, a butterfly, and the symbolic mask of the earth god.
Both pieces are from the famous treasure found in tomb 7 at Monte Albán, which was used anew in Mixtec times. Gold work is practised only by the late civilizations of ancient Mexico, and most of the original examples of this craft are found within the orbit of Mixtec civilization, generally considered as the workshop of fine craftmanship.

90 PAINTED CLAY VASE, with three supports in the shape of serpents' heads. Mixtec Culture. Height, 25.5 cm. (10 in.). British Museum, London.
The mythological figures, distributed over the surface in a purely decorative manner, and picked out from a dark red background in black, white and orange, show the stylization also found in the pictographic illustrations of Mixtec codices. Mixtec ceramics,

though simple in form, are decorative in their gaily coloured patterning and the lustrous glazes of their vases. Their influence is particularly predominant also in the late ceremonial pottery of the Aztecs.

91 THE PYRAMID OF TENAYUCA. Portion of the front with stairway.

92 SIDE VIEW OF THE PYRAMID, with snake sculptures lining the lower terrace.
In its present form, which probably dates from the year 1502, this pyramid, situated on the northern edge of the city of Mexico, is the fifth superstructure covering a considerably older, pre-Aztec edifice. The Aztec version of the pyramid is impressively sober and severe. The double stairway is by now becoming an established feature, corresponding to the twin temples usually erected on top of the platform. The stone ornamentation is confined to snake sculptures, let into the walls of the pyramid and surrounding the basement of the building.

93 COLOSSAL STATUE OF COATLICUE. Basalt. Height, about 260 cm. (102⅜ in.). Museo Nacional, México, D.F.
Coatlicue, the terrible death goddess of the Aztecs. With her apron of knotted snakes, her breast adorned with human hearts, hands and skull, her serpent hands and the two snakes which rise from her headless trunk as symbolic spouts of blood, joining to form a new face of superhuman violence, she also embodies, in this representation, the triumph of Aztec sculpture which could handle a theme of this kind in such a masterly fashion. The statue was found in the vicinity of the main temple of Tenochtitlán which is today the central square in the city of Mexico.

94 RELIEF OF A HUMAN SKULL, representing the initial of the period in the calendar year which is dedicated to the god of death. Basalt. Height, 40 cm. (15¾ in.). Museo Nacional, México, D.F.
The relief is carved into one of the sides of the memorial to the "Holy War" which was consecrated in 1506–7 and is one of the chief works of Aztec ceremonial sculpture.

95 BASALT FIGURE, with emblems of the god Xipe. Height, 56·6 cm. (22¼ in.). Private Collection, Mexico, D.F.

96 BACK VIEW of the same figure.
To honour the god of spring, Xipe, priests covered themselves with the skins of victims who had been flayed in the service of his cult. The statue here shown, which is dedicated to this fertility ritual, does not share the terrible, rigid inexorability of the great sacred sculptures, but rather testifies, in form and detail, the unconstrained realism shown by Aztec sculptors whenever they were free to rely on direct observation from nature. The scars on the chest mark the sacrificial cut; the back of the head and back show where the skin worn on top has been knotted together.

97 MALE HEAD in grey tufa. Height, 18·3 cm. (7¼ in.). Museo Nacional, México, D.F.
This is one of the rare sculptures in which eye and mouth encrustation have been completely preserved. It consists of reddish and yellow shell, with polished pyrites for the pupils. The head was found in the centre of the city of Mexico.

98 SQUATTING FIGURE, wearing the mask of the wind god across the mouth. Basalt. Eyes encrusted with obsidian. Height, 39 cm. (15⅜ in.). Museo Nacional, México, D.F.
In their cubic stone carvings Aztec sculptors achieved a masterly balance of vigorous outlines. Note how the religious "subject" of the sculpture, the mask of the wind god, Ehecatl, becomes the dominant element and artistic centre of the composition.

99 WOODEN FEMALE FIGURE, with traces of eye and mouth encrustation in shell. Height, 38·8 cm. (15¼ in.). Museo Nacional, México, D.F.
Very little of the old Mexican wood sculpture, which must once have been of considerable importance, has come down to us. Apart from richly carved Mixtec and Aztec wooden drums, only a few figures carved in wood exist and these do not make it possible to judge the degree of influence which wood sculpture had on sculpture in general.

100 OBSIDIAN VASE in the shape of a monkey. Height, 13·7 cm. (5⅜ in.). Texcoco. Museo Nacional, México, D.F.

101 CROUCHING MONKEY with ear pendants. Basalt. Private Collection, Mexico, D.F.

Among the most attractive works in Aztec plastic art are the animal sculptures. These are free from the mannerisms of ritual art and full of an originality and creative exuberance. The monkey vase, chiselled out of volcanic glass and polished to a high gloss, is a master-piece also in the technical sense; the product of an ancient tradition in the working of a material which is very plentiful in Mexico.

102 MASK OF XIPE-TOTEC, god of spring. Basalt. Height, 21 cm. (8¼ in.). British Museum, London.

103 BACK VIEW of the same mask.
The oval swelling round the mouth indicates that the face of the god has been covered with the skin of a sacrificial victim. The full figure of the god is carved into the back, a feature which is peculiar to Aztec masks representing divinities. The style of Aztec stone masks follows the tradition originally set by the Teotihuacán sculptors, but they reproduce the full oval of the face, including the hairline.

104 ROCK CRYSTAL SKULL. Length, 20·8 cm. (8¼ in.).
105 British Museum, London. Front and side view.
The genuine old rock crystal carvings which we know today date mostly from the Mixtec and Aztec periods. This wonderfully luminous, life-size skull from the British Museum is the most important specimen of its kind.

ACKNOWLEDGMENTS

I wish to express my grateful thanks to all those Museums and Private Collectors who gave me permission to photograph the works of art reproduced in this book and who were so ready to offer their assistance. In particular I should like to mention the "Museo Nacional de Antropologia", the "Instituto Nacional de Historia e Antropologia", the Department of Ethnography of the British Museum in London, as well as Sres. Miguel Covarrubias, Diego Rivera and Franz Feuchtwanger in Mexico.

I. Groth-Kimball